WEEKEND
WITH
JESUS

MICHAEL EDWIN Q.

WEEKEND
WITH
JESUS

Published by: ADVANTAGE BOOKS™
                   Longwood, Florida, USA
                   www.advbookstore.com

Library of Congress Catalog Number: 2018967182
1.   Fiction: Christian - General
2.   Religion: Christian Life - Inspirational

Editor: Nancy E. Sabitini
Cover Design: Alexander von Ness

First Printing: December 2018
18 19 20 21 22 23 24   10 9 8 7 6 5 4 3
Printed in the United States of America

One

Thursday Night

The word *Ordinary* sounds so ordinary. However, there comes a time in every life when ordinary sounds just fine. It soothes the mind and nerves. To stand at the bow seeing a clear sky and calm waters is what all sailors wish for. An adventure is only called an adventure after the fact. At the time of its passing, it's considered an inconvenience at the least, dangerous at its worst.

George and Martha were ordinary. Their lives were predictable, which gave them a feeling of security. They lived in a cozy house on a modest street in a safe, comfortable neighborhood in a peaceful little town in Midwest America. Their love for each other was strong, without question.

They filled their days with details. Time flies for those living with details. But time could never diminish their love. Sweethearts since high school, nothing in that department has changed. Though looking at their old prom pictures you could see the changes the years made. They both are a little plumper. Martha started to dye her hair dark, covering up the gray sprouting out of the sides of her head. George is doing a comb-over, covering up the balding spot on the back of his head, just like his father before him. Still, to look at them most folks would say they were attractive, ordinary, but attractive.

Avid churchgoers, both George and Martha held strong belief in God and country. Though secretly they felt they needed to do more, but life's filled with details, and details filled their days.

Yes, George and Martha were ordinary; they wouldn't have it any other way.

At the end of each day, when George comes home from work, Martha always likes to have a pleasant dinner waiting for him. They sit, taking their time, enjoying each other's company, catching up on the details of the other's day.

Though Martha always fetches the mail from the mailbox out front at three in the afternoon, early morning on Saturdays, she never opens any of it. That's George's job. Not for any other reason than he enjoys doing it, where as she couldn't care less.

"Bills, bills, and more bills; that's all we ever get!" George complains as he sorted through the daily post.

"If it's not bills, it's some charity looking for a handout!" Martha adds.

"Hello, what's this?" George holds up one of the envelopes to the light. "Must be some kind of joke? Here, look."

Martha takes the envelope, holding it up to the light. "A handwritten letter...so what about it?"

"The return address, look at the return address!" George points to the top left-hand corner of the envelope.

Martha reads out loud, "Jesus the Christ...Right hand of the Father...Heaven." She hands it back to her husband. "I've got to give them credit; those charities are getting more inventive everyday. Open it up; I've got to hear this one."

George examines the letter carefully.

"So, what does it say?"

"This must be a joke," George mutters.

"So, what's it say?"

"It says, 'Will arrive Friday night at eight thirty for a weekend visit. I can't wait to see you both.'"

A look of bewilderment and wonder washes over George's face.

"Is that all?" Martha asks.

"Just the signature," replies George. "It's signed, 'All my love...Jesus!'"

For some unexplained reason, George places the letter against the flower arrangement in the center of the kitchen table. He knows it to be foolishness; he knows the better choice is to toss it in the garbage; but he doesn't. Martha watches him; she knows she needs to question his action; but she doesn't.

"It's a scam," George declares.

"How...? Martha questions.

Returning to his dinner, George sums up his suspicion, "It's to get our attention. It's probably for a magazine subscription or something."

All through dinner, they stare at the letter; only taking their eyes off it long enough to cut their food.

"So, how was your day?" George asks.

"What's that?"

"I asked how your day went."

Martha sits mesmerized by the letter.

"Martha!" George puts a little more vigor into his voice.

"Oh...what's that, darling...did you say something?"

"Never mind, it was nothing."

He takes another bite, joining her in staring at the letter.

"So, how did your day go?" Martha asks.

****

Martha pops another cashew into her mouth. She relaxes in her armchair; her show is coming on, a weekly television spectacular, professionals judging amateur dancers and singers, what have you for big prizes. The show's opening music starts; a loud noise is coming from the other end of the house shattering her concentration.

"George, what are you doing?" she hollers.

His voice comes from the den, "Where's the family Bible?"

"The Bible…what do you need a Bible for?"

"I want to look something up; have you seen it?"

"How should I know; where did you put it last?"

The show is starting; Martha begins feeling agitated.

"Have you looked in the bottom drawer of the desk?" she shouts down the hall.

"Yes, but it's not there."

"Did you check the drawer in your nightstand in the bedroom?"

There is a long silence; she hears his footsteps tramping into the bedroom – another long silence.

"I got it!" George's voice ricochets back.

"Good for you," Martha says under her breath. It is good timing; the first contestant is about to perform.

****

"Will you turn off the light and go to sleep?" Martha complains, sandwiching her head between two pillows. George is still thumbing through the Bible.

"It says here, Jesus is coming again to claim his kingdom, the second coming," George proclaims.

"That's right, except first there's supposed to be a drawing up into the clouds with him," Martha replies.

"You don't say? Where does it say that?"

"I don't know; it's in there somewhere. The book of *Revolution*, something like that! I don't know. It's the last book of the Bible."

"You mean, Revelation?"

"Yeah, that's it! Now, shut off the light and go to sleep!"

"Just give me another minute. I can't sleep till I figure this out."

"Whatever!" Martha tightens the pillows across her eyes.

Two

Friday Morning

Groggy from the night's sleep, George and Martha tumble out of bed, stumbling about the bathroom. Martha wraps a housecoat around her, runs a comb through her hair, and brushes her teeth. Her first concern is sending George off to work with a good warm breakfast in him and his brown bag lunch in hand. Once he's on his way to work, she'll shower and dress for the day. George, on the other hand, lays out his clothes for the day on the foot of the bed, then enters blindly into the shower. The blast of cold water brings him to a rude awakening. His eyeballs bulge from their sockets.

In the kitchen, Martha puts on a pot of coffee. She takes George's lunch, which she prepared the night before, packing it into a brown paper bag. She fries three sunny side eggs, two for George and one for her, a few strips of bacon, and buttered toast. She hears George coming from the bedroom. That's her cue to pour the coffee.

"Morning, sweetheart," George announces as he sneaks up behind her, putting his arms around her, pulling her in close, kissing her cheek. She smiles, giggling; she likes the attention he gives her.

"Morning, dear," Martha coos. "Sit down; everything's ready and still warm."

Sitting at the table, they find the letter still propped against the flower centerpiece. During the night they'd forgotten about it, yet now the sight of it floods their minds. Neither George nor Martha mentions a word about it as they eat their breakfast. Like the night before while eating dinner, they are under its spell. It still has a mesmerizing affect over them. They stare at it constantly. They stare at it over their coffee, over their sunny side eggs, and over their toast and bacon.

"What's your plan for today?" George asks.

To his surprise, Martha answers, never once looking at him, her eyes remain glued to the envelope at the center of the table. "I don't know, I was thinking I might straighten up the guest room."

"Why, is your sister coming for a visit?" he asks, figuring it the only logical answer. The only time Martha ever straightens the guest room is when her sister visits.

"No, I just thought it a good idea, in case we ever have some unexpected guests."

Unexpected guests…? George thinks. *We never have unexpected guests.* In all the years of their marriage never once did this happen.

He looks at the letter and then at Martha. She looks at the letter and then at George. They look at each other, thinking.

"We are acting so silly," George declares. "A simple envelope is throwing us out of whack. It's just an ad or a scam."

"Yeah, but wouldn't it be the best thing in the world if the letter were true?" Martha whispers. Then she thinks twice, "Then again, wouldn't it be the worst thing in the world if it were true?"

George sees her point; if it were true, it could go either way. Such thoughts lead to self-examination, not always a pretty sight.

He rises from the table, leans over to kiss Martha one last time before leaving.

"Don't forget your lunch," she warns.

He grabs the brown paper bag as he scoots out of the kitchen. Martha gets up, starting for the front door to see him off. Instead of making his way to the front door he rushes back down the hall to their bedroom. It confuses Martha, but she says nothing, wondering what he's up to. A few seconds later, he's flying out of the bedroom and down the hall. He's holding his lunch in one hand and something in the other.

"You're taking your Bible?" Martha questions when she recognizes the not-so-used black book he carries.

"Yeah, I thought I'd read it on breaks and during lunch," he says as he flashes past her and out the door.

She shrugs her shoulders, thinking *Why not. Reading the Bible is a good thing. It wouldn't hurt me either to do the same.*

George's Friday Morning

At the front door, George kisses Martha good-bye. He walks to his car that's parked on the street. Before opening the door, he takes one more look toward his home. Martha still stands in the doorway, holding her housecoat close around her. He waves to her; she kisses her hand, blowing it in his direction. She enters the house, closing the door behind her. Twenty-five years of marriage has not changed his feelings for her. She is still the most beautiful woman known to him, the love of his life. For Martha, he will always be her one and only, the love of her life.

Driving away, he looks in the rearview mirror at his home. The sight of it fills him with pride. True, it's no mansion, but it's a nice little house. He thinks back to their frugal days when they first married. They were in their twenties, living in that tiny shabby apartment not far from the college he attended. He remembers the sacrifices they made, mostly those made by Martha. He feels blessed. They've come a long way since then. In comparison, their small home *is* a mansion.

He drives the speed limit down streets he's driven thousands of times before. His destination is the Continental Building. Only today, something is different. Instead of his usual brown bag lunch resting on the passenger seat next to him, there is something else. His usual tuna fish salad sandwich, an apple and chips (Martha always makes him fish on Friday…something to do with a song she once heard) – instead, there rests his Bible. He took it with him, determined to find the answers to the questions swirling in his head.

He thinks back to his childhood. Church, prayer, religion has always been a part of his life. Martha was the same. She was the one who insisted on a Church wedding. After that, they became members of the local Church, missing only a few Sunday's in all those years. It all seemingly made some sense to him, only lately the pieces didn't seem to fit. There was something missing in the equation.

Sadly, strangely, all those years of Church going has not brought him any comfort, nor the confidence he so desires. The Bible is as much a mystery to him as it was when he was a boy. In his youth, he spent endless hours reading the Bible. It sounded so holy and right, yet never clear to him. He can tell you what he believes, but not why he believes. Heaven forbid, he finds himself called on to defend his faith! He fears ever having to meet those demons with such poor armor and such little weaponry.

He looks over at the Bible next to him. In some strange way it gives him comfort, just to have it near. Even stranger is the feeling he is not alone, as if someone were sitting next to him. Stopping at a red light, he reaches over, placing his hand on the book. There is comfort in that, too.

****

Coming out of the elevator, George smiles, nods, grinning at everyone he passes.

"Good morning…good morning…good morning," he says nearly a dozen times or more before he gets to his work area.

In his work cubical, George places his brown bag lunch in the bottom drawer of his desk, placing his Bible next to a framed photo of Martha. He turns on his computer, preparing for the day's work. George likes his job, somewhat. He enjoys the work and the challenge. Nevertheless, still something is lacking for him. Every one of his coworkers likes him and he likes them, yet there's a distance between them all that George so desperately wants to cross. He wonders if the others feel the same way. It's a subject that's never mentioned. There is an even greater gap between the workers and management – the all-seeing eye looking for fault in everyone.

Twenty three years, four months, twenty-six days and George will be up for retirement – but who's counting. There are worse things in life than drudgery.

****

He's a dark figure of a man, tall, lanky. Stewart Dennison likes being in charge – in charge of his office, in charge of his wife and children, in charge of his entire life. Even as a child, he enjoyed being the one to call the shots – to be in control. He learned at an early age how to control people around him. From childhood to the present everyone called him by his last name, Dennison, never Stewart. It seemed better fitting for him. His father had been hard on him growing up; but now, thinking back, he realizes it was a good thing. Nothing is more unattractive in a man than weakness. Dennison is hard as a rock.

10

His hair well-groomed, styled not just cut every week. His suits are the best that you can get off the rack, fine quality and expensive. He dreams of the day he can wear custom-made suits. He knows it will happen. He's never failed to achieve what is in his sights. It's only a matter of time and effort.

To rule over all you survey, one must have certain qualities. A person needs their character to be stronger than other's. That is the key. There is no room for abstract or fantasy; everything must be solid and concrete. The only faith that matters is to have faith in oneself. The only belief is to believe in one's self. Anything else is for the weak. To believe in anything other than oneself is to live with a crutch that's a handicap of one's own making. Stewart Dennison felt little pity for those who afflicted themselves in such ways; swearing never to be one of them. He took pride in his philosophy, obviously the only alternative as he saw it. To make your mark on this world, in this life, is the most important thing.

****

Midmorning, a knocking on the front panel of his cubical disturbs George's concentration. He looks up; it's Dennison, his supervisor.

"Sorry to bother you, George. Could I have a minute; I'd like to see you in my office."

George doesn't say a word. He follows closely behind Dennison to his office. George tries to read between the lines, the tone in Dennison's voice. He thinks: *I get all my work done on time. I don't think I've made any major mistakes. I'm never late, hardly ever miss a day. What could it be?*

Dennison's tone is not a friendly tone, clearly serious, yet not severe to suggest something is wrong. George gives out a sigh. He's tired of trying to second guess Dennison.

"Close the door, George, and sit down," Dennison says, gesturing to the chair in front of his desk as he sits down.

A smile appears on Dennison's face; instead of offering a feeling of relief for George it causes him more confusion. He's smiling, which he seldom does, is not something Dennison is known for. The smile is friendly, although the tone is still serious. Nothing is making sense to George. Mentally, he raises his hands and surrenders. Whatever will be, will be, just like the Doris Day song. Besides, walking on eggshells was never one of George's strong points.

"So, George, how long have you been with the company?"

A strange question to ask, George knows Dennison knows the answer. Perhaps it's some kind of test. He better answer.

"Nearly ten years, sir."

Dennison sits back in his chair, folding his hands, placing them on the desk.

"Happy here, are you, George?"

Quick! Think of a good answer.

"Yes, I am," was the best George could do, he felt it would suffice.

"Good…that's good…we like our employees to be happy."

"Is there something wrong, sir?"

"Wrong? No…nothing's wrong, not exactly." The word *exactly* digs into the back of George's skull like a hot poker. Dennison takes a moment before continuing. "George, I like to think we've known each other long enough to call each other *friend* and I can speak to you in confidence."

Oh, oh, here it comes.

"Of course…?" George responds, only he secretly thinks they've never been friends, at least as far as George understands the term.

"It's about your desk."

"I know it's untidy, but…"

"That's not what I'm talking about, George. I'm talking about what's on your desk."

"You mean my picture of Martha?"

Dennison laughs at the thought. "No, no, the picture of your wife, no, that's okay. It's the book."

"You mean my Bible?"

"Yes, your Bible, George. I'm afraid it goes against all company policy. You understand; there's the law of separation of church and state. I believe it's in the Constitution or something."

George falls dumbfounded, silent.

"You need to understand how offensive it can be to some people who work here. We don't want a scandal, now, do we? We've got Hindus working here, Muslims, Buddhists, and I don't even have to mention all the atheists. It's offensive, George."

George shakes his head. He's never heard of such a thing, nor has he ever thought about it. This is coming from far left field. He doesn't want to offend anyone; except doesn't he have rights, also.

"I'm not saying you can't read it on your own time, in the privacy of your own home. Just think of all the people you're offending. If not for them, think of me!"

George remains silent. His mind is racing so fast, none of the words he'd like to say ever slow down enough to make it to his mouth. Then again, if he did, he might be digging his own grave.

"So, do everybody a favor, keep the book at home?" Dennison smiles at George.

"I suppose I could…"

"That's the spirit!" Dennison interrupts. "I can always depend on you, George."

"I understand, but…"

"That's good, George. I knew you'd understand."

A feeling of frustration flows through George's veins as Dennison continues spouting off what he believes to be correct.

"I must say though, George, I'm a bit disappointed. I always thought of you as a levelheaded person...a modern thinker."

George looks at Dennison with confusion. "I don't understand."

"Don't get me wrong," says Dennison. "I've read the Bible, myself, several times. I found it moving, full of good solid morals. Don't kill anybody, don't steal, don't litter, I'm all for that. But all those outlandish and bizarre fables, not to mention all those contradictions, a thinking person can't take it seriously!"

"Fables...contradictions...like what?" George asks.

"Well, like...like after Cain kills his brother and he's forced to skedaddle. He leaves with his wife! Now tell me, where the heck did his wife come from?" What did she do just pop right out of the air? It sounds a little weird to me."

George shrugs his shoulders, not knowing. A feeling of shame comes over George. He should know this stuff, but he's defenseless.

"What about Noah and the ark; you seriously believe the entire earth was underwater? I mean no boat is big enough. If all that's true, what happened to all the plant life?"

George shrugs again, falling deeper into self-loathing.

"Jonah caught in the belly of a whale for three days. That sounds like something straight out of a fairytale. Kind of fishy don't you think?" Dennison stops for a moment to laugh at his pun. "Fishy, get it?" He continues, "Burning bushes...seas splitting...virgin births...walking on water, they're all sorts of myths, legends, and folklore; and what about the dinosaurs?"

George no longer bothers to shrug his shoulders. He knows there are answers, but he has none. More shame comes over George.

"We've come a long way since those dark days of superstition! Science gave us the answers. Any up-to-date homo sapien with half a brain could never fall for such childishness. I say, grow up and get a life!"

George realizes that without knowledge of the Bible a Christian is left standing like a fool, and George feels foolish.

****

Back in his cubical, George removes his Bible from his desktop, putting it away in the bottom drawer. He takes his brown bag lunch out of the drawer, placing it next to the picture of Martha. Her smiling face makes him feel even more ashamed of himself. He let down God, himself, and now even Martha.

George feels confused, disappointed. Confused because so much of what Dennison said made perfect sense to him if you look through the eyes of the world. Nevertheless, deep down inside, he knows Dennison is wrong; there are answers to every one of his questions. Only George doesn't know any of them. He feels low in himself with just a hint of bitterness.

"The pastor at our church, he'd know the answers. If only the pastor was in the room he'd show Dennison what for." George says to himself, except he knows in his heart it is no real excuse for him not knowing.

Three

Martha's Friday Morning

At the front door, Martha kisses George good-bye. She waves as he drives off to work. She watches through the window till his car turns the corner. There is a silence so severe when George leaves. It's so thick you can cut it with a knife, a stillness bearing down on her. She would think after all these years she'd be use to it. But it's the same every morning. She must contend to it anew.

If they had children, perhaps there would be a welcomed noise about her. They tried for years to have children with no success. Test after test, the doctors had no answers. There really was no cause for it. It is a God thing, and He knows best. Though there are times a person would like to argue the point just like Job.

Years into their marriage they seriously considered adoption. They went through the motions, but again God intervened. They were blocked at every turn. Sometimes they were too late, other times too soon, but never at the right place at the right time. The child of their dreams always slipped through their hands.

Martha thinks how nice it would have been. She'd clear out the guest room, paint it blue and pink, put in a crib, and fill the room with stuffed animals. If it was a boy, she'd want it to be just like George; if it was a girl...?

George came from a small family as did she. He was an only child. Martha never met George's father, he died when George was twelve. His mother never remarried, raising him on her own. Martha only met the woman a handful of times, once being at the wedding. She lived one state over, hated to travel, enjoying living on her own. When she became deadly sick, she and George discussed having her move in with them. Although before they could act on it, she passed on in her sleep. George was heartbroken, taking a year or more to put it behind him.

Now, for Martha, there is only her sister, Eileen, who lives one state over with her husband, Bob, and her two boys, Jeff and Tommy. They seldom get to see one another. It is such a treat when they do visit. Having her nephews around is a joy, both bitter and sweet – all the noise and the running around.

Martha is filled with love. It overflows from her. It would have been nice to have someone else in her life to shower them with the spill over.

Back in the kitchen, she pours another cup of coffee. Sitting at the kitchen table, staring out the window at the back garden, she wakes back to reality.

"Enough of this," she says aloud. "Nothing's going to get done today staring into space thinking about *What if*."

She rises, cleaning up the kitchen. Then it's back to the bedroom to wash and dress for the day. She's just about to step into the shower when the phone rings. She wraps a towel around her, rushing into the bedroom where she picks up the phone on the nightstand. She doesn't even get the chance to say *Hello* when a voice takes over.

"Martha, it's me, Jane. What are you doing for lunch, today?"

"I don't know…the usual sandwich. Why do you ask?"

"That's right, I forgot, it's tuna salad Friday," laughs Jane. "You're a predictable creature of habit, Martha."

Martha doesn't respond; sometimes it's best not to say a word when it comes to Jane. Sometimes it's best to just let her have her say and shrug it off.

"I'm going to make a drop off at the church, you know, the food drive. If you're doing the same, we could meet for lunch."

"The food drive, is that today?" Martha asks.

"Of course it is, silly; don't you remember? Today is the last day; you have to get it there before noon. That's why I thought we could have lunch. Let's say, Lillian's Tearoom at noon?"

"That sounds fine, Jane. Listen, I'm standing here freezing with just a towel on. Let me get ready. I need to put a box together for the food drive."

"You mean you haven't put it together, yet? I did mine a week ago."

Of course, you did, thinks Martha.

Jane continues, "Well, hop to it, girl. These food drives are heaven-sent. If the church didn't have them twice a year, I don't know if I'd ever clean out my food cupboard."

"I know what you mean," Martha agrees. "Listen, Jane, I need to hang up. Let me get ready. I'll see you later."

"Later!" Jane sings, before she hangs up.

****

Martha adores Jane – always has, always will. Friends as far back as High School, Martha always looked up to Jane. She was always so sure of herself, not like Martha who was constantly in a flux, unsure of her every move. In school, Jane was head cheerleader, captain of the volleyball team, working on the school paper. Martha, on the other hand, was everything Jane wasn't; she found what little light she could in the shadows.

And the boys, they all were crazy about Jane. If not for Jane's popularity, Martha seldom dated. She'd catch the overflow of boys surrounding Jane. Not that Jane was one to share. She always felt that any boy who showed interest in her belonged to her. If any boy showed interest in any other girl, that would be Jane's next venture, to steal him away from her. No boyfriend was safe from Jane. Sometimes Martha thinks it was a good thing she met George after Jane married, or she would probably gone after George. These are the things a friend of Jane endures.

Martha grew up feeling insecure around most people. Only with George did she feel capable, confident. That was one of the things that attracted her to him, one of the things she loved about being with him. With George she felt beautiful, able to perform any task with confidence and ease.

Still, after all these years, in Jane's presence, Martha is awkward, tongue-tied, all thumbs.

****

Once dressed, ready for the day, Martha takes an empty cardboard box from the garage, and then begins rummaging through the kitchen pantry. There's a can of peas, an excellent source of protein. Last time peas were on sale, she bought way too many. Two jars of beets. What she was doing with beets she didn't know, neither she nor George liked beets. Two bags of marshmallows she planned to use last Thanksgiving, only she never did. A box of *Coco-Critters Breakfast Cereal* she bought the last time her sister and her family came for a visit. She figured her nephews would enjoy something like that in the mornings. However, never was it opened after her sister warned that much sugar put into her boys was like lighting a fuse on a powder keg. They would be wired for the day and probably not sleep that night. There was a package of *Little Willie Cupcakes*, and *toaster pasties*, also too much sugar for a child. There was a package of *Lady Choy's Fried Chinese Wonton Noodles*, from when she experimented in oriental cooking. A can of *Cream Corn* rounded out the dry goods. Finally, a bottle of *Forbidden City Duck Sauce* and a container of *Jamaican Curry Powder* with an expiration date that was two years past due. In fact, looking at the expiration dates on all the items, only the canned goods were still acceptable.

She places the cardboard box in the back of the station wagon, heading off towards the church.

Four

James and Darcy

Meadow Lane Community Church is James Monroe's dream come true. His father was a pastor. Saved at an early age, James couldn't think of a time in his life he didn't want to grow up to be like his father and become a pastor. When he was in high school it looked inevitable to both friends and family. He was also popular in school, a good speaker and debater. He worked well with others, being on the wrestling team and captain of the swimming team. His marks were high, putting him in the top ten of his gradating class.

Being in the ROTC, after graduation he joined the army. There it was the same; he was well liked, always on the advance. On base he was a help to the chaplains, running a Bible study in the barracks.

When his military service was up, receiving an honorable discharge, he knew it was time to follow his one true calling. He enrolled in seminary.

All through seminary school he prayed for an assignment to such a Church as Meadow Lane Community. It is a small, close-knit family church where everyone knows everyone else, caring and working together. Now, everyday in his prayers he gives thanks for all God's gifts and Meadow Lane Community Church is high up there on his list, right under Darcy, his wife.

Darcy Kelly had been his childhood sweetheart. They lived and were raised on the same block. Of course, James went through the early phase of not liking girls. His first memory of her is him pulling her ponytail, she retaliating by throwing mud pies at him. This phase in life didn't last long, and they began to see each other in a different light. In no time, they were like two peas in a pod, always together. Both James and Darcy hold no memory of a time they did not want and know their destiny was to marry each other. It was clear in Darcy's mind. They'd marry, James would become a pastor. They'd have kids, a house, living forever happy.

Their plan was to wait for James to graduate seminary school and settle in a Church before marrying. But young love is impatient; they married after his first year of school. This didn't sit well with their parents and family. Still, the faith everyone held in this young couple, plus a church wedding healed all wounds; little was voiced about the matter.

It was difficult, the next few years. They lived in a small garage apartment, walking distance from campus. Sacrifice filled their lives; he sacrificed for her, she for him, both of them for their God. It was all a question of faith. They had a strong faith for each other and for what they were doing. Though use to a finer way of life, Darcy never once complained. She believed in her husband – she still believes in James.

After James' graduation, they still lived in the same small apartment. They had little if any prospects. James worked for a delivery service, leaving early in the morning, returning late in the evening. He worked six days a week, often on Sundays, which didn't sit well with him, but it was that or no work at all. Darcy waited on tables at a local café. Though she did her job joyfully, James found it difficult to see her work so much, so hard. The way some people treated her, he vowed one day things would be better; she would never have to work so hard, again.

James sent out letters of introduction to churches in the state. The letter stated his qualifications and his life's intentions. Dozens of typed bios lay ready on his desk to mail to those churches interested in him. For months, no one took any notice. The bios began to collect dust, turning yellow. Finally, out of the blue, he received a letter from Meadow Lane Church asking for more information. He sent a more detailed bio.

Eight months after his graduation, James received an offer for the pastor position at Meadow Lane Church. It was the answer to all their prayers. They praised the Lord with newfound joy.

The move was an easy and quick one, they had such few things. That was ten years ago, neither James nor Darcy regret their decision, nor does the church for making the offer. It is a perfect fit all the way around

Happiness abounds, for them, for the Elders of the Church, for the congregation, for the community as a whole. The only ones to feel any disappointment were the single women of the congregation. Many a hope dashed silently against stone to see such a young and handsome Pastor, discovering he was already taken. However in time, even *they* warmed to this new couple as the others did. They began to trust the new Pastor who gives of himself to all without question, with all his heart. As well, to his lovely wife, the woman behind the man, the woman at his side who seemed cut of the same cloth.

****

Martha is a block away from the church to deliver her food drive drop-off when she turns the corner, immediately seeing something is wrong. She slows down, finally parking the car, turning the engine off.

Next to the church is the home where Pastor Jim and his wife, Darcy, live. There is an ambulance parked out-front. Martha sits in the station wagon a half-block away, watching. A paramedic team wheels out a gurney carrying Darcy Monroe. Pastor Jim follows close behind. They pile into the back of the ambulance; a moment later driving off with no siren or lights flashing.

Martha turns the key, drives to the front of the church and parks. She carries the box of groceries to the Monroe home, intending to leave it on the doorstep. The door opens; it's Linda, the church secretary.

"Martha, you just missed it," remarks Linda. "You know how ill Darcy's been. Well, she's gotten so bad; they needed to take her to the hospital. Poor dear can't even sit up straight or the Pastor would have driven her; they had to wheel her out and take her in an ambulance. They just left."

"An ambulance…?" Martha echoes, trying to sound surprised.

"Yes, an ambulance…the poor dear," says Linda. She looks at the box Martha is holding. "Oh, you must be here for the food drive. Here, let me take it."

"It's not much," Martha confesses.

"Oh, don't be silly, we welcome every donation. God bless you, Martha. See you in church."

Walking back to her car, Martha wonders about Pastor Jim and his wife. She wonders what she would ever do if something ever happened to George.

****

Entering Lillian's Tearoom, Martha sees Jane sitting at a corner table waving her over.

"I hope you don't mind," says Jane. "I'm in a hurry; I have to get back soon; so I ordered for you. You do like salad?"

"Salad's fine," Martha says, not wanting to make a scene.

"Martha, darling, you look white as a sheet! So, what's wrong…George seeing another woman?"

"Jane, where do you get such notions? The way your mind thinks, it scares me. No, I just came from Church; they took Darcy Monroe away in an ambulance."

"Well, it doesn't surprise me in the least," Jane goes on. "The life of a Pastor's wife must be a nightmare."

For the next half-hour, Jane goes on about what is wrong with the marriage of the Pastor and his wife. She also points out the flaws in the marriages of the Nelsons, the Garrisons, the Petersons, and the Andersons. She gossips about who is presumably stepping out on whom, apparently lying to whom, assuming robbing from whom, and seemingly unfaithful to whom.

Martha drives home full of presumably, apparently, seemingly, possibly, maybe, and hearsay. Enough gossip, she thinks her head will explode.

Five

George's Friday Afternoon

At lunch, he'd planned to read his Bible. He knew for certain he had that much right. Only after the scene with Dennison, all the fight is knocked out of him. He quietly ate his lunch alone. At the end of the workday, George shuts off his computer, stacks all his unfinished work in a pile, ready for Monday. Opening the bottom drawer of his desk, he removes his Bible.

Walking to the elevator, other workers wish him a goodnight. He says nothing, just silently waving good-bye. In the parking lot, he gets into his car, placing the Bible on the passenger's seat, the same place as that morning.

Driving home from work, George reflects on his day. He finds it interesting how a few short hours can change everything. That morning, he drove to work with his Bible next to him with all those hopeful feelings welling up inside of him. Now, driving the same streets, with the same book next to him, he feels nothing. No...not anything...he feels alone.

He expects what Martha is making for supper. It is always the same. Every Friday she takes the remaining tuna fish used for the tuna salad sandwiches and makes tuna noodle casserole. It's all so predictable just like his entire life...predictable.

An uncontrollable sensation takes hold of him, the urge to stop. He sees a park up ahead. He sits in his car, looking at children playing, their parents sitting on the benches, watching over them.

Surprisingly, even to him, he feels jealous. Not of the parents who are blessed with children, a prayer never answered for Martha and him, but jealous of the children. They run around with so much energy, chasing one another, playing games, riding the swings, climbing the monkey bars, so free and alive. The smile leaves his face.

"Is this all there is to life? Stacking days up till there aren't anymore? There's got to be more!" he whispers to himself.

He turns the key; the engine roars thankfully drowning out his thoughts. He drives home, taking care to go the speed limit.

As he parks the car out front of their house, he vows to change his mood. There's no need to bring Martha down with him. He needs to be optimistic for her. He draws in a deep breath, slowly exhaling all the negativity.

Opening the front door, he hears the sound of pots and pans clashing in the kitchen. Martha prepares the casserole like every Friday.

"I'm home!" he shouts to the kitchen.

Dear, sweet, Martha. No matter how down he feels there is always one bright light...Martha. The smile returns to his face.

Six

Martha's Friday Afternoon

The oven beeps a signal when it reaches the needed temperature – 350°. Martha places the casserole dish on the middle shelf, bringing back from the fridge all she'll need for the green salad.

It's her mother's recipe, not that there's much to a tuna noodle casserole. Except there are a few ingredients most people don't use. Add a little dry mustard to the mix with garlic and onion powder, top off with paprika for color. Lastly, when it's done, take it out of the oven, letting it rest for a few minutes. Then when you're ready to serve, spoon it on the plate, giving it a few sprinkles of dill. It adds to the richness.

Every time she prepares this dish, she can't help thinking of her mother. She tries to remember what her mother looked like. Funny, how even the face of your mother can become vague and faded in your memory over time. She remembers her sister's voice was nearly the same as their mother's, at least in the way she frames her words. A strong impulse surges up in her to call her sister.

"Hello?"

"Eileen, it's me, Martha."

"Martha! Is everything all right?"

"Everything's just fine. I just wanted to hear your voice."

There is a long silence from Eileen's end of the line.

Finally, she speaks, "That's so sweet. I'd love to talk with you, too. Only the kids are running through the house with the dog, I haven't even started on dinner, and the drier's buzzing. It's not a good time. Maybe we can talk when life isn't such a nightmare. Got to go, love you."

The line clicks dead.

Martha thinks *a nightmare*? That's a nightmare she has only dreamed about since she married George. The phone call has made her feel worse, more alone. *Oh, where is George?*

Looking for the dill in the cabinet, she reflects on her day. The vision of Darcy Monroe being wheeled to an ambulance is foremost in her mind. *The poor woman, perhaps she should call the church and ask if there's anyway she could be of help? Perhaps that would be too forward? Besides, that's a job for someone who knows them better.*

She thinks back on all the gossip Jane told her during lunch. It swirls around in her head, leaving her dizzy. Then again, she never stops Jane from spewing gossip, nor does she ever question her on the source. Is it all just hearsay based on nothing? Then it occurs to Martha the reason she never questions Jane is because she enjoys it. That would make her a gossip, too, wouldn't it?

She takes down the dill, placing it on the counter. Her hands are shaking

"Is this what life's all about? Sticking your nose in other people's business! The days passing by swiftly till one day you're dead! There's got to be more!"

The question frightens her. She thinks back on all the wonderful sermons she's heard Pastor Jim give in church. She should know better, and she knows it. Still, that doesn't stop her. The question finds it mark, its hurts.

Just then, she hears a car pull up front; she looks out the window. It's George. She thinks *George works hard everyday without a complaint; he deserves more than coming home to a grumbling wife*. She forces a smile onto her face. Looking in the mirror she pats her hair into place as she adjusts her clothes. She wants to look her best.

Looking out the window, she watches George come up the walkway.

Dear, wonderful George…such a good man…I should be grateful. Thank God, I have George.

Seven

Friday Night

George lazily pushes the noodles around in his plate with his fork. His eyes rest on the letter still propped against the centerpiece.

"It'd serve us right if He did come for a visit," George mumbles under his breath.

"You said something, dear?" Martha asks.

"No, I was just thinking out loud; it was nothing." George thinks for a moment, he decides to share his feelings. "Really, what I was saying was 'It would serve us right if He did come for a visit'. I don't know what I'd do or say; I've got so many questions. Besides all that what would He think of us? I mean, I don't think of us as bad people, yet I don't always feel like I'm right with the Lord. Today, my boss walked all over me, and I let him. He literally tried to tear my religious beliefs apart, and I let him. No, I didn't let him; I allowed it, because I had no defense. I'm Biblically ignorant. The Bible tells us God loves me. Then why can't I love me? It's very confusing."

Martha takes the plates, resting them in the sink. "Would you like some ice-cream?" she asks.

"No, thank you; I guess I'm not hungry, tonight."

Martha sits down again, taking hold of her husband's hand. "I understand how you feel. I guess I feel the same way. I want to do what's right; only I don't always do what I say I'm going to do. It's all too confusing."

A solemn look comes over George; he takes his time before he answers.

"Martha, you know I love you."

"Of course, I do." She tightens her grip on his hand. He continues.

"Lately, something's happened, things making me look harder at myself, at us. I'm not happy with me or the way our lives are going...there's got to be something more." He points to the letter. "What if it was true? What if Jesus walked through our front door this minute?"

"You're a good man, George; I don't want you putting yourself through this. You've got nothing to be ashamed of."

To George's amazement, she takes the letter; walks to the trash can, dropping it in.

"What are you doing?" he questions loudly.

"Enough is enough. There! Now that's the end of that!"

Just then, the doorbell rings. They both shoot a look at the clock on the kitchen wall. It's eight-thirty, just like the letter predicted. They look into each others eyes. There's an unspoken excitement in the air.

"You don't think?" George asks.

George dashes to the front door, Martha follows close behind. He stops just short of the door, turning to her.

"What if it is Him?"

"Don't be silly, that's ridiculous!"

"If it's so ridiculous, why did we both rush to answer the door?" He gently pushes the curtains apart, peering out.

"Well, who is it?" Martha demands.

George spins round, eyes wide. "It's Him!"

"What are you talking about?"

"It's Him…it's…it's…it's Jesus Christ!"

"Oh, that's nonsense! Out of my way!" Martha pushes George aside, looking out the window.

"It must be a joke, it's got to be. It's someone in a costume selling magazine subscriptions. It can't be…"

She takes hold of the doorknob and looks to George for guidance. He nods the go-ahead. She opens the door. All expression leaves her face; her skin turns pale; she stands motionless as if turned to stone, or worse, a pillar of salt.

Standing in the doorway is a young man in his thirties. He is wearing a long white robe and sandals. His hair is shoulder length; his full beard nicely trimmed. From head to toe, he is the image of what most people agree as the image of *Jesus Christ*. An image any talented actor with the aid of a good makeup kit and costuming could portray, save for one characteristic, the holes in his hands and feet. With close inspection it's clear these are not theatrical tricks. The wounds are real. George thinks of the apostle Thomas – Doubting Thomas. That moment of epiphany Thomas experienced is now the same for Martha and George.

However, it's not the look of Him or even the holes in his hands and feet convincing George and Martha this indeed is the Christ; it is his eyes. If the eyes are the window to the soul then you can only imagine what George and Martha found themselves confronted with.

Martha feels a weakening in her limbs, an urge to fall to her knees. Jesus catches her in his arms; as she goes down, He holds her holder up.

"There's no need for that," He says. "I'm not here on official business; just a friendly visit, that's all."

When it is clear George and Martha are speechless and can do no more than stand and stare, He takes the initiative.

"I'm tired; mind if I just go straight to my room?"

"Oh, no, of course, right this way," George says, gesturing toward the guest room.

Jesus tows a small white duffel bag at his side. George reaches out for it.

"Thank you, but I can handle it," Jesus says, smiling at George.

In the guest room, Jesus places his duffel bag down, looking the room over, wearing a look of contentment.

"I'm sorry we don't have anything better to offer," Martha says as she fluffs up the bed pillows.

"No, this is great, just great! You can't imagine how much this means to me," Jesus says, sitting on the edge of the bed. He looks around once more, smiling at Martha.

"You've fixed it up nice. You have a flare for such things, Martha, one of your many talents. I like it."

"You sure you want to go to sleep, now?" George asks. "I mean, we've got so many questions to ask you."

"I'm sure you do," Jesus says. "How could you live all these years with all those questions? It must have been difficult for you?"

George feels an urge to reply, "Difficult, indeed", but holds back his tongue. He wonders how many of the questions could be answered if he just looked a little harder.

Jesus stands and starts gently ushering them out of the room. "I'm so tired. Traveling long distances always does me in. If you don't mind; we can talk in the morning."

George and Martha stand in the doorway wearing questioning faces in wide-eyed confusion.

"Is there anything special you'd like for breakfast?" Martha asks, not sure why she thought such a question relative at the moment. She just felt a need to say something and that's what came out.

"Do you have any grilled fish?" He asks, smiling.

The request takes Martha off guard. She wants to say yes, but she can't see how.

"I can have George go over to the fish market early in the morning," Martha declares.

"They don't open till ten," George adds, thinking the conversation a bit too strange.

"Please, don't do anything different for me," Jesus says. "What do you normally eat in the morning?"

"I usually make pancakes and coffee on Saturday mornings," Martha replies.

"You eat cake in the morning?" Jesus asks.

"It's not really a cake. It's more a bread, only it's sweet…a sweet bread."

Jesus gives her a questioning look. Martha realizes what she said.

"No, that's not what I mean. It's not Sweetbreads; it's bread that's been sweetened."

Jesus smiles understanding. "No need to change for me; that sounds just fine."

"I think there's some tuna casserole left in the fridge," she replies, again feeling foolish after what she just said registers in her mind.

"Pancakes will be fine. Now, if you will please forgive me, I'm tired." He slowly closes the door.

Before the door closes, George tries to get in one last question. What he feels is an important one. "Is this the second coming?" George asks in a tone of declaration.

"No...no...not even close; like I said, this is unofficial, just a friendly visit. If this were the second coming, you'd know it. Now, if you don't mind, I don't mean to be rude, I'll see you both in the morning."

George and Martha stand silently for a moment. Then without one word, as if hypnotized, they march to their bedroom. Martha stops midway down the hall.

"Do you think He knows?" Martha whispers.

"Knows what?" George asks.

"Never mind, of course He knows."

"Knows what?"

"Stuff...?"

"Martha, I don't even understand what you're talking about."

"Neither do I," Martha says. "I feel like I'm going crazy."

"Crazy...what do you mean?"

"What do you mean....what do I mean? I mean the Lord of Lords, King of Kings; the Prince of Peace is sleeping in my guest room. I'm going to make him pancakes in the morning. I'm supposed to act like nothing strange is happening out of the ordinary, go to sleep and then wake up in the morning and make pancakes for Him. That's what I mean!" She realizes she's beginning to repeat herself. That's not a good sign.

George nods, agreeing.

"Do you think He's real?" she whispers.

"I would think so," George says. "I mean, if you saw Him and I didn't, I'd say you were crazy. And if I saw Him and you didn't, then I'd say I'm crazy. But since we both see Him, I'd say He really is here."

"Or we're both crazy," Martha adds.

"Or we're both crazy," George echoes.

Martha nods, agreeing.

"I guess there's nothing else to do but go to sleep and see what the morning brings," he says, walking slowly toward their bedroom with Martha close behind.

After turning off the lights, they lay in bed staring up at the ceiling they cannot see in the dark. Hours pass slowly; neither George nor Martha sleep a wink.

Eight

Saturday Morning

Breakfast

The following morning, George and Martha rise earlier than usual. They wash up, then dress in a daze, not speaking, not even the usual "Good morning". They find their way to the kitchen. Martha puts on a pot of coffee, laying out all she'll need to make breakfast. Once the coffee is done, they sit at the kitchen table nursing their cups, lazily as they do every Saturday morning.

"Should we wake Him?" George asks.

"That is if there is a Him," Martha says. "We might have both dreamed it."

"How can two people have the same dream?" he asks.

"Maybe, we both dreamed we had the same dream," she says.

"That's confusing," George remarks. "I don't know which is more frightening, going in and seeing no one there or seeing Jesus. Either way, I'm not ready for this. I don't know if I can handle it."

Just then, they hear the door to the guest room open; they hear footsteps in the hall. Their bodies stiffen, they wait. Suddenly, Jesus appears at the kitchen doorway.

"Good morning, everyone," Jesus says as He enters the kitchen. They instinctively begin to rise when He enters. "No, don't get up." He says, placing his hands on their shoulders, pressing them down into their seats. "I told you this is an unofficial, informal visit."

Jesus continues silently standing before them, smiling. It takes a moment for George to realize what's happening. Jesus is waiting to be invited to sit.

"Oh, please, have a seat," George says, gesturing to one of the chairs.

"Thank you," Jesus says taking the seat near the window.

George thinks to himself, *why would the creator of the universe need my permission to do anything?*

As if George spoke out loud and not in his head, Jesus answers his question. "It's a matter of respect and good manners. Yet more than that, I seldom go where I'm not invited and welcomed."

The couple stares at each other, motionless, speechless. Finally, Martha rises from her seat, walking to the stove. "Would you like some coffee?" she asks Jesus.

He looks around, pointing to a glass pitcher. "Some orange juice sounds good, if you don't mind?"

The three sit quietly, sipping. Suddenly, Jesus starts to laugh.

"It just dawned on me," He says. "George and Martha...you're names are George and Martha!"

"I know, we get that all the time...George and Martha Washington," George says.

"No, that's not what I was thinking," Jesus says. "George and Martha...they're the two main characters in Edward Albee's play: *Who's afraid of Virginia Wolf?*"

"You like Edward Albee?" George asks.

"Edward Albee, a bit too depressing for my taste. And the vulgarity, well, you know how I feel about that, still the man has talent!"

The three fall back into silence and their sipping. Martha places three plates on the table, one for each of them. Each plate has some scrambled eggs and a short stack of pancakes. She would usually make bacon, but not today. *It's a Jewish thing*, she wonders, *He is a Jew, right? I mean, He still is, right?*

George plants his fork into his pancakes when he catches a side-glance from Jesus. "Oh, grace, I'm sorry. I forgot. Would you like to say grace?" he asks Jesus.

Jesus remarks, "No, George, this is your home, your table. I would say the responsibility falls squarely on your shoulders."

George and Martha bow their heads, folding their hands. George is not sure what to say. He decides on something short and to the point. "Dear Lord, for what we are about to receive, make us truly thankful. Amen."

Somewhere inside George he knows he needed to say more. Only, to his relief, Jesus doesn't seem displeased with him.

"So, these are pancakes," Jesus says, eyeing his plate.

"They're best with syrup over them," George says, pointing his fork at the bottle of maple syrup.

Jesus pours syrup over his pancakes, slices a piece with his fork, putting it in his mouth. He remains silent as he chews slowly.

"So, what do you think?" George asks.

Jesus chokes out one word, "Sweet..."

"Yeah, ain't it great?" George agrees with pride.

Just then, the loud sound of a lawn mower pierces the stillness.

"That man!" Martha exclaims, looking out the window. "A person can't have five minutes of quiet! Every Saturday morning it's the same; he's out there mowing his lawn before you can get your first cup of coffee down!"

"Who is he?" Jesus asks.

"That guy across the street in the Bermuda shorts and the silly black socks, him with his ridiculously loud lawn mower."

Jesus rephrases his question, "No, I mean, what's his name?"

"Don't know," George replies. "We just call him that guy across the street in the Bermuda shorts and the silly black socks."

"So, you don't know his name?" Jesus emphasizes, looking out the window at the man mowing his lawn. "Do you know if he's saved?"

"Saved…?" George asks, sounding thrown off his guard.

"Yes, you know…saved. You do know what I mean when I say saved?"

"Yes, of course I do," George answers, sounding embarrassed he didn't get the gist of the question right off. Secretly hoping Jesus doesn't ask for a full definition. "Saved…? I'm afraid I don't know; I've never spoken with the man."

Jesus looks up and down the street from the open window. "How many neighbors do you have; and do you know if they're saved?"

"I couldn't say that either," George responds, his eyes gazing to the floor.

"There's that one young couple next door! One time I saw the husband getting in his car; he had a Bible in his hand," Martha quickly points out, hoping to lighten the air. "At least, I thought it was a Bible," she sadly adds.

"Or a copy of Moby Dick," Jesus says knowingly.

"We just don't want to be bad neighbors," Martha draws to a close.

"No one could ever accuse you of being bad neighbors," Jesus says, reaching across the table, placing his hand on Martha's. He reaches for his orange juice. He takes a sip; a large smile appears on his face. This sends a feeling of relief through George and Martha. "So, what's on the agenda for today?" He asks, looking at Martha.

"Well, I need to do some housework; then later some of my girlfriends are coming over in the afternoon for tea, we have a book-reading club."

"That sounds great! What about you George?"

"Oh, I was planning on doing some errands around town; then I need to stop by the office to get some papers I need to review."

"Mind if I come along?" Jesus asks.

"Of course not," George replies; there's a nervousness in his voice.

"Great!" Jesus announces. "I hope we can be back in time for Martha's tea party."

"Oh, usually, when Martha has her girlfriends over for a get-together, I try to stay out of their way. I've got a little woodshop set up in the garage. I'm working on a desk, right now. Know anything about woodworking?"

Jesus smiles, "Yes…a little."

Nine

Jesus, George and Dennison

To George's surprise, not a single one of his neighbors mowing their lawn pays any mind to Jesus as they get in the car.

"Nervous, George...?"

"A little...I mean...how am I going to explain you to people?"

"The same way you've always explained me to people."

That is a double-edged answer, if George ever heard one. He decides he's better-off keeping his mouth shut. Except he realizes no one is giving them a second glance. "Can they not see you?" George asks.

"Oh, they see me all right; except each person sees through their own eyes; they see things the way they want to see them. It's the same thing with their hearing. They hear what they want to hear." Jesus smiles at George. "Don't worry, George; there won't be any trouble, I promise you."

It's true; not one person shows any hint He looks out of place. Still, He does not go unnoticed. His sheer presence seemingly has a strange affect on people. Simply being near Him brings out each person's inner self – only more intense – more noticeable.

If a person is normally friendly, they are even more friendly than usual. If they are the joyous type, they thoroughly bubble with joyfulness. On the other hand, if a person is normally rude or crabby, they come across as downright hateful. Though many seem content to be near Him, others become fidgety, looking as if they hold back a strong urge to run away. It is different nearly everywhere they go, and with every person they meet. Though He speaks hardly a word; He touches the heart of everyone He comes in contact with.

Shopkeepers go out of their way to be accommodating; salespeople smile sincere smiles; while some storeowners can't hustle them out fast enough, slamming the door behind them. It's no different for the world as a whole, Jesus always affected the world. It's how people act towards Him that makes the difference.

George parks near the front door of the Continental Building; the car parked next to his belongs to Dennison.

Good, Dennison is here, George thinks.

"This is where I work," George announces. "I need to pick up some papers to review for Monday. Would you like to see where I work?"

"No, that's all right; I'll just wait here in the car," Jesus says, to George's disappointment. This is his chance to show up Dennison. George shows up with the big guns, but the guns refuse to fire.

"No…really…come upstairs with me; I'd feel honored if you saw where I work." There's a hint of desperation in George's voice.

"Very well," Jesus says, "if it means that much to you, let's go see where you work."

Who am I kidding, George thinks. *You can't hide anything from God, so why try? But if he knows, why doesn't He call me on it?*

The two enter the building and into the elevator; George presses the button for the third floor.

"I know what you're up to, George," Jesus says, smiling, shaking his head.

Oh, oh…here it comes.

"I'm not up to anything Lord; I just want you to see where I work."

Why am I saying this? It's like I have an instinct to do and say what's wrong. This is crazy.

"Very well," Jesus says, "we'll play it your way."

What's most disturbing is George knows he's lying. What's worse is he knows Jesus knows he's lying. Still for some unexplained reason he can't help himself. He can't help thinking how Dennison put him on the spot; how he wished Pastor Jim was there to answer all of Dennison's questions and make him look foolish. Only this is better than Pastor Jim; here is the Living Christ in the flesh to address all of Dennison's issues – He will tear Dennison to shreds!

George places a few papers into a folder, tucking them under his arm.

"This is my cubical; I know it's not much…"

"A picture of Martha…" Jesus exclaims, picking up the photo. "You know, I'm so glad you have each other."

"I do love her," George proclaims.

"Yes, she is lovable," Jesus agrees, placing the frame back down. He turns to face George, looking him squarely in the eye. "Dennison is in his office; that's why you've asked me here?"

"I'm sorry, Lord; it is true," George admits, sounding embarrassed.

"Don't feel ashamed, George; I understand. Besides, it all works out for the glory of the Father; you'll see."

Dennison hunches over his work at his desk. George gently taps on the door.

"George…what are you doing here?"

"I have some papers needing review before Monday; I came by to get them. Looks like you're burning the midnight oil?"

"Yeah…it's never done," replies Dennison.

George backs away, giving Jesus room to enter.

"This is a friend of mine that I'd like you to meet. Dennison…this is Jesus…Jesus…this is Dennison, my boss."

Jesus enters the office. George wonders how Dennison sees Jesus. It seems his vision is nothing out of the ordinary. He barely blinks when he looks up from his desk, smiling up at Jesus – that business smile, friendly but not familiar.

George thinks, *Now sparks are going to fly!*

Jesus stands front and center before Dennison's desk.

"So you're a friend of George?" Dennison asks.

"Yes...why, hasn't he ever mentioned me to you, before?"

"No...I don't think he ever has. Why...should he?"

"Yes, he should have; it's important."

Not understanding the answer fully, Dennison looks at Jesus oddly.

"Well, it's a pleasure to meet you. Now, if you two gentlemen will forgive me, I must get back to my work."

"Of course, I understand," Jesus says, heading for the door.

What? That's not the way this is supposed to go.

"See you, Monday, George," says Dennison, picking up his pen once more, returning to the papers on the desk before him.

Jesus leaves the office, followed by George.

No, stop, don't leave, yet!

Out in the hall, George approaches Jesus.

"Lord, I don't understand."

"What don't you understand? You wanted me to slay the dragon for you; but I didn't. Wasn't there enough done for you? This isn't my job, George, it's yours." Jesus' tone is still friendly yet firm.

"I don't know what to say," George pleads. "I just freeze up when people question my beliefs. Where do I start?"

Jesus smiles and whispers, "Like they say, every journey, no matter how long or short, near or far, starts with the first step. Will you take the first step, George?"

George stands for a minute, thinking. Then, he turns, taking position in the doorway of Dennison's office. He taps lightly on the door to catch Dennison's attention. Dennison puts down his pen, looking up.

"Yes, George?" asks Dennison.

"Mr. Dennison, I was doing some studying, and there is no amendment in the Constitution about separation between church and state."

"There isn't?"

"No...I've looked at the company rule book, there's nothing that says I can't keep my Bible on my desk, as long as I read it on my own time."

"Interesting," says Dennison. "So, George, what are you trying to tell me?"

"I'm trying to say if we are friends like you say how about we have lunch together next Friday?"

"Why?' asks Dennison.

"Well, for one, you said we were friends. Shouldn't friends have lunch together every now and then? Second, I've got a two-for-one coupon for McCormick's Steak House. I'd hate to see it go to waste. And third, I'm tired of tuna salad sandwiches every Friday!"

Dennison breaks into a hearty belly laugh. "Sounds good… you and me… McCormick's… next Friday. It's a date. See you Monday, George."

"See you Monday," George says, turning from the doorway.

Halfway down the hall, Jesus stops in front of George. "You've taken the first step. I'm proud of you, George."

"You know, I'm proud of me, too." An impish grin forms on George's face. "It's a shame though."

"What's a shame?" Jesus asks.

"If you confronted him, you would have blown him clear out of the water."

"Perhaps, except don't you know, George, if I blow him out of the water, he'll never learn to swim.

Ten

Jesus and Walter

Walter Alistair has a plan; it's not a great plan, but it'll do for now. All his life, Walter's code was "Do onto others before they do it to you". Not that you should kill someone or harm them; that would be wrong. Although, bending the rules isn't the worst you could do to them. What people don't know won't hurt them.

Where does a person get such ideas? Now that's a good question. Certainly not from his mother or father, they weren't that kind of people. In fact, there was nobody in Walter's past you could point a finger at. It was strictly Walter's idea. Again, how does someone get that way? Just look within. All of us have something. How did we get here?

Whenever Walter bent the rules, a little voice in the back of his head told him he was doing wrong. Usually, it was his mother's voice, but sometimes it was his father's. Yet, other times the voice was his own, a small voice, easy to extinguish. Like a small spark that could turn into a flame, it never did. Walter suppressed it quickly.

He'd remember how poor his parents were, always scraping to get by. For all their goodness there was no reward. No one he ever met who was well-off lived their lives as his parents did – the so-called moral way. He swore on the day he left home he would never be a sucker like them.

He learned early what a person does and says makes a difference in the outcome. So, why not do and say what is sure to be beneficial on your own behalf.

"Too good is no good," he would always say. "A person has to take his life into his own hands and mold it; and not let anyone or anything get in their way."

When that little voice showed up, he'd push it back down – far down as he could, burying it as deep as possible.

Captain of his own ship, master of his life, and slave to no one, he vowed each night and each morning.

Sure, he wasn't anybody special, at least not yet. He'd gone from job to job, each time going further down the ladder. But he was still young. He knew eventually his lucky break would come. He just had to keep on keeping on with his plan and his ways.

He will not always be a no-body – this he vowed.

****

George stops the car at the local gas station.

"We need gas," George announces, turning off the engine and getting out. After filling the tank, he pops his head into the car window. "I'm going inside to pay. I need gum; is there anything you want?"

"I'd like water, if it's not too much trouble."

"One bottle of water coming right up," George says, making his way toward the convenience store.

A moment later, George is back in the car; he hands a bottle of water to Jesus. Jesus hands it back.

"Hold this for me, please. There's something I need to look into."

George doesn't say a word as Jesus gets out of the car; he feels it isn't his place to question.

Inside the convenience store, the young man behind the counter steps forward.

"May I help you, sir?" he asks.

"Hello, Walter."

The young man smiles, looking a bit uncomfortable, "How do you know my name? Do I know you?"

"Not yet, but you will."

"Say, is this some kind of joke?" Walter laughs nervously. "What do you want from me?"

"I just want to ask you a question."

"A question...?'

"Yes, a question, strictly hypothetical...no strings attached."

"Go ahead, I'm game," Walter says through a crooked smile. "Ask away."

Jesus moves in closer till Walter's face is inches from his.

"If someone wanted to buy your soul, how much would you charge?"

"This is a trick question, isn't it?" asks Walter.

"No trick...strictly hypothetical, mind you...if someone wanted to buy your soul, how much would you charge?"

A serious look washes over Walter's face; he thinks for a minute. Then he smiles when the answer comes to him.

"It wouldn't happen...if somebody wanted to buy my soul, it wouldn't happen. Nobody has that much money!"

"How is that?" Jesus questions.

"Because...my soul...is...priceless!" Walter proclaims with pride.

"You don't say?" Jesus sounds astonished. "I'd have thought there must be some amount you'd sell your soul for."

"Well, there isn't! What did you think I was going to say, a *Billion Dollars*?" There's a touch of sarcasm in Walter's voice.

"No, I was thinking of an amount a bit lower."

"Oh, yeah; like what?" Walter's sarcasm grows.

"The amount I was thinking of was one dollar and eighty-three cents."

The smile falls from Walter's lips, all expression leaves his face. His hands begin to tremble; his heart starts racing. A fear like none he ever knew in his life comes over him. Not only is he caught in a lie, Walter is sure the man standing before him sees right through him, knowing every sin he ever committed. No…even worse…the man witnessed every sin he ever committed, no matter how private. There is no place for Walter to hide, not even within himself.

Walter jumps over the counter and runs out the door. He taps on the driver's side; George rolls down the window.

"Excuse me, sir; but you forgot your change." Walter hands over to George one dollar and eighty-three cents.

"Well, thank you, young man."

"Don't mention it, sir."

Walter dashes around the car and holds the passenger door open for Jesus.

"So, Walter, you know what you need to do next?"

"Yes, I do!"

"Good…" says Jesus as he gets in the car. Before Walter closes the door, Jesus smiles at him. "I love you, Walter."

Walter feels as if his heart is melting.

"I love you too, Lord," says Walter as he shuts the door. He waves good-bye, watching through tear soaked eyes as the car pulls away and out of sight.

Back in the store, Walter takes the phone out from under the counter and dials.

"Mom…? It's me…Walter."

Eleven

The Book Club

Back home, George finds no place to park in front of the house – the members of Martha's book club snatched all the spaces. He parks in the driveway behind Martha's station wagon.

"There's a side door to the garage; that way we don't have to go in through the house," George says.

He flicks the lights on in the garage revealing a top-of-the-line professional wood workshop.

Jesus takes in a deep breath. "Don't you like the smell of wood?"

"That's just what I think every time I come in here," George admits.

Jesus holds up a handful of sawdust up to his nose and smiles.

George takes pride in his workshop. He loves showing it off. "Here is my lathe…my band saw…and my sander…"

"Is this the desk you're working on?" Jesus asks.

"Yeah…that's it. A few more hours of sanding and I'll put on the first coat of stain."

George bends down, eyeing the angles of the desk; then he drops his head and gently hammers his head down on the wood.

"I can't believe how stupid I can be at times. Here I am asking you if you know anything about working in wood. It just dawned on me…you were…I mean…you are a carpenter. I guess I just wasn't thinking."

"Don't be so hard on yourself, George. You had several things on your mind at the time. Besides, though I did make my living as a carpenter for a time, what makes you think I was even any good?"

"You would have to be…I mean…."

"I appreciate the reverence, George. But remember, I'm just a man…just like you. I put my pants on one leg at a time, just like you; that's if I wore pants."

The two men begin to laugh.

"If you must know the truth, I wasn't a good carpenter…I was great!"

Their laughter grows louder.

Jesus looks around the workshop. "I didn't have anything near as fine as this workshop. You're a blessed man, George."

"Yes, I am," George agrees. "First, blessed to know you…" The smile leaves his face, as he turns serious. "To know Martha is the blessing of my life. This workshop is why we both park on the street. There are plenty of women, if their husbands wanted to set up a workshop in the garage, they'd say *no way*. Sweet Martha, she's never complained once." George stares starry-eyed at the door connecting the garage to the house.

"I told you before she was lovable," Jesus says.

"That she is," George takes pleasure in saying so.

"I wonder how she's doing with her book club?" Jesus asks. "George, you wouldn't think me too rude if I went into the house and looked into how the meeting is going?"

"No, not in the least, I'm sure she'd be glad to see you."

Jesus heads toward the door leading into the house.

"By the way, George, that desk is coming along great."

"You think so?"

"Yes, I do."

****

Entering the house, Jesus walks down the hallway toward the sound of voices. He finds the small group in the living room. Martha and four other women sit in various chairs; a tea service rests on the coffee table.

"I hope I'm not disrupting anything?" Jesus asks as he enters the room. "It's just I'm interested in books myself."

Martha looks up, startled, jumping to her feet like a soldier coming to attention when the commanding officer shows up. The other women look at her strangely and then at her houseguest.

Martha regains her composer, yet remains standing, "Oh…everybody…this is our houseguest, Jesus," Martha announces. "Jesus, these are my friends, Jane, Terry, Mimi and Phyllis."

Jesus smiles at them all, nodding for Martha to sit and relax. The women remain confused over Martha's reaction to this stranger. What does he have on her for her to act so peculiar?

"Jesus…is that a Spanish name?" asks Jane.

"No, it's the Latin form of a Greek name."

"Oh, Greek," coos Phyllis, "Such passionate people the Greeks." She directs her next statement to the other women. "I just love Greek food. Have you ever eaten at *The Olive Branch* downtown? It's simply divine."

"No, I'm not Greek…I'm Jewish."

"Oh, Jewish," says Jane, sounding a bit pompous. "Are you a relative?" she asks, wondering if there's any Jewish blood in Martha or George's family tree.

"No, I'm just a friend."

"From school?" asks Phyllis.

"No, I'm a childhood friend."

"Oh, really?" says Jane sounding suspicious.

I suspect Martha never talked about me to any of you?" Jesus asks.

They all shake their heads.

"No, wait," says Mimi. "I think I remember once she mentioned you to me."

"Oh, did she?" Jesus says, smiling at Martha.

"Only I don't remember what she said. I think it was last Christmas. In fact, if I remember correctly, it had something to do with Christmas. I think…I honestly can't remember."

"Oh…that's too bad," Jesus says with slight remorse. Then He changes the subject. "If you don't mind, I'd like to sit in. I'm curious about what happens during a Book Club get-together."

He sits next to Mimi on the sofa, across from Jane.

Though there is no leader to their Book Club, Jane takes the leadership role, as usual, to explain the rules. "Well, first we vote on what book to read," says Jane. "We read it at home. Then we meet in a week to discuss it…critiquing, as we like to call it."

"So, you read an entire book in a week?"

"Yes, we just finished discussing this week's book. We were about to select a new one, when you came in," says Terry.

"What was this last book about?"

"It's called *Love out of Breath*," responds Jane. "It's about the life and loves of Alexis Heartily. It begins with Alexis leaving Drake Morgan, the billionaire oilman from Texas."

"Excuse me," Jesus interrupts. "You say she left him…where did she leave him?"

"On his ranch in Texas, where they were living together," says Mimi.

"Then you're saying there was no marriage between them?" Jesus tilts his head slightly to one side.

"No, they weren't," Terry breaks in. "But that wasn't the way Alexis wanted it. Drake kept insisting she sign a prenuptial. Of course, she refused. She's not stupid; she's her own woman."

"So why did she leave him?"

"Because, she found out he was seeing someone else," explains Phyllis.

"So what's wrong with seeing someone else?" Jesus asks.

"Not seeing with your eyes seeing," responds Jane. "He was sleeping with another woman. He was cheating on her!"

Jesus tilts his head to the other side. "Don't misunderstand; I don't condone what Drake did. He's obviously thinking only of himself and no one else. But if there was no marriage, how can you call it cheating?"

"Well, I don't know what they call it where you come from," insists Jane. "They had an understanding. Where I come from, cheating is cheating!"

"So, this so called understanding they had together binds them?" Jesus asked with a hint of confusion.

Jane looks at him as if He is a misguided ten-year-old.

"What happens next?" Jesus asks.

"She moves to Hollywood," says Terry. "She becomes a top model. She winds up on the covers of all the major fashion magazines. In no time at all, she becomes rich. Of course, she meets other men…a photographer…even a movie star. Only they can't compare with Drake, her first true love."

"Does she have an understanding with these men, like she did with Drake?" Jesus asks.

Terry answers, "No, these were just your everyday hello-good-by type of relationships, nothing serious."

"I see…I think"

Phyllis adds to the story, "Eventually, Drake tracks her down and tries to win her back, but she still refuses to sign the prenuptial."

"Then it happens," Jane takes over. "A car accident…Alexis loses control of her car, slides off the road and into the Pacific Ocean. The accident leaves her horribly disfigured. That's when we see Drake's true colors. He visits her in the hospital. Only now that she's no longer beautiful, he doesn't want her. Without so much as a good-bye, he heads back to Texas. Alexis is heartbroken. Not to mention she'll never model again."

Terry adds a portion, "All those other men…the photographer and the others, they want nothing to do with her either."

Phyllis takes the story from there, "It takes most of her riches to pay for the plastic surgery to regain her beauty. That's where she meets Robert Nelson, Hollywood's top plastic surgeon.

"During her convalescences, the two fall in love. And here's the good part. He falls in love with her while her face is still wrapped in bandages. He falls for her, not her looks and not her money – that's gone, anyway. When they remove the bandages, she is more beautiful than ever. And, just when you think everything will be okay, it goes bad. You see, although Robert is living in a loveless marriage, he's afraid to leave his wife because everything is in her name.

"Except when Alexis opens a successful beauty salon on Rodeo Drive, and becomes wealthy again, things change. They now have enough to start fresh, and he leaves his loveless marriage. He and Alexis run off to marry in a small chapel in the south of France. And they live happily ever after!"

A questioning expression appears on the face of Jesus.

"Forgive my ignorance, there's one point I don't understand. If Alexis left Drake because he was 'seeing someone else'; because he was a 'cheater', why would she marry a man who was a 'cheater'?"

"Because he was in a loveless marriage and theirs was *True Love*," Jane states plainly. "You men are all alike; you don't get it! Love is what counts! Love is the most important thing in life!"

Fearing the direction the conversation is taking, as well as feeling uncomfortable and slightly ashamed, Martha speaks up.

"Why don't we vote on this week's book?" she announces.

"What books do you like?" Jesus asks.

"Oh, all kinds," replies Terry. "We like romance, espionage, murder-mysteries, just about everything."

"Might I suggest a book?" Jesus asks as he rises from the sofa. He rushes off to the guest room. He returns with a black, leather-bound book; he rests it down on the coffee table.

"What's this, *Moby Dick*? I'm not much for the classics, myself," says Jane.

Mimi pushes her fingers across the gold lettering on the front of the book.

"It's not Moby Dick…it's the Bible!" she says.

"The Bible…you've got to be kidding?" exclaims Jane.

"Why not the Bible…?" Martha demands. "It has everything we look for in a book! Besides, maybe we might learn something!"

Jesus smiles his approval at Martha.

"I vote we read the book we considered earlier," Jane proclaims. "All those in favor of reading *Live for Tomorrow* raise your hands."

All club member's hands go up save for Martha's.

"There, that's settled, we read Live for Tomorrow." Jane raises her arm, eyeing her wristwatch. "Oh my, look at the time, I must run. Next get-together is at my house. See you there!"

"It's been a pleasure to meet you," says Jane looking at Jesus as she stands.

"Yes, a pleasure," says Terry.

Phyllis nods and smiles.

In a flash, Jane is out the door, followed by Terry and Phyllis. Only Mimi lags behind. She reaches across the coffee table, placing her hand on the Bible.

"Does it really have in it all those things you mentioned?"

"That and more," Martha answers.

"Gee, I've always wanted to read it," Mimi confesses.

"Then you should."

"Here, you can have my copy." Jesus hands the book to Mimi.

"Oh, I couldn't," says Mimi. "You don't live around here. How could I ever get it back to you?"

"I'd consider it an honor and a privilege if you kept it…a gift to you from me. Besides, I have other copies. I even have a first edition signed by the author."

"Do you?" coos Mimi, sounding impressed. She clutches the book to her. "Thank you, I'll treasure it always." She stands, smiling at Jesus, "Well, nice meeting you."

"It's great meeting you, too," Jesus replies.

When Mimi is gone, Jesus starts toward the guest room. "You know, I'm proud of you," He says to Martha.

"That means so much to me," Martha replies. "Say, you were only joking when you said you had a signed, first edition copy of the Bible...weren't you?"

Jesus smiles one more time at Martha, before he disappears into the guest room.

Twelve

Saturday Afternoon

Lunch

"I like them; I really do!" Jesus exclaims, sitting with Martha and George at the kitchen table.

"It won't hurt my feelings if you don't; I'll cook you something else if you like. It's just you mentioned you like fish; this is the best I have in the house to offer."

"I'm enjoying them, honestly. Now, again, what do you call these?"

"They're called fish sticks."

"Interesting; how do they get them so straight and squared off?"

"Modern technology," George replies.

"Oh…" Jesus nods his head slightly.

"Perhaps, for dinner, we can get some whole fresh fish; but I can't think who sells it. There isn't a fish market for miles; and what the super market sells is never fresh. We're so far from freshwater and the sea," Martha says.

"Dinner…that's got me thinking," Jesus says.

The way He said He's been thinking sends Martha and George into a panic. They've come to realize being a follower of Jesus is a position of action. Your life can't be stagnating if you're a follower. Though Jesus is mild mannered and unassuming, just being around Him is demanding, sometimes even without a word said. So when they hear the words, "I've been thinking", they know it's time to make ready for something – God only knows.

"You tell me you don't know who your neighbors are or if they're saved. Now is a good time to find out; and what better way than to invite them over for dinner."

"Dinner…tonight…but I don't know what I could serve them?" There is a noticeable panic in Martha's voice.

"How about making *Babylonian Layered Surprise*?" Jesus replies.

"It sounds exotic," Martha says. "Babylonian Layered Surprise…how do you make that?"

"Well, you preheat the oven to 350°, and then take a casserole dish and grease it real good so nothing sticks. Then you take your ingredients forming the layers. First layer is two jars of beets, covered with one can of peas and one of corn. The next layer is wonton noodles mixed with toaster pastries and cupcakes and then sprinkled lightly with a box of Coco-Critters. Finish it off with a layer of marshmallows, some Duck Sauce and dust freely with Jamaican Curry Powder."

Martha looks as if she is about to cry.

Jesus takes her hand, leans toward her and whispers.

"Don't be upset. That's not why I spoke. I want you to learn and grow. What have you learned, Martha?"

Martha takes a moment to reflect.

"If a person is hungry, they need and deserve a meal; not my throw-away scrapes. That's not what I would eat. If it were, it wouldn't be in my cupboard, it would have been eaten." She looks at Jesus. "Love thy neighbor as thyself?"

"Now you've got it!" Jesus places his hand on hers, "Again, I'm proud of you." He smiles; she smiles back. Jesus turns, looking to George. "George, I saw a grill out in your backyard; does it work?"

"Like a dream," George responses.

"Good...we can serve grilled fish. Don't worry about the fish, I'll supply that. First, let's find out how many guests we are to have."

"How are we going to get them to come?" George questions.

"Simple, we go door to door and invite them."

"But we don't know these people."

"That's the point. Isn't it, George?"

George nods agreeing.

"What if they don't want to come?" Martha asks.

"Then they don't come. But you'll never know until you try."

"If they do come, where will we fit everyone?"

"The backyard is large enough. We'll have a picnic."

Martha and George do not look or feel enthusiastic, they stare at Him blankly.

Jesus rises from his chair smiling down on both of them, excitedly. "This is going to be such great fun," He announces.

George and Martha come to the clear realization they don't share in Jesus' definition of what fun is.

****

After lunch, the trio head out into the neighborhood. Martha and George are hesitant, moving slowly. Jesus runs at full steam ahead.

"We might as well invite the lawn mowing guy across the street in the Bermuda shorts and the silly black socks," George says, pointing to the house.

"Best not," Jesus says. "He's fast asleep right now. He works nights; that's why he mows so early in the morning. He does it as soon as he gets home; it's the last thing he does before he showers and goes to bed. Let's start with the house next to his."

For the next two hours, they go from house to house inviting neighbors to a backyard cookout that evening. Each time they ring a doorbell, George and Martha become stiff with tension. If no one answers, they instantly relax. But as a door opens, they look like two deer in the headlights.

Some people are not home; others look out their windows, refusing to open their doors. Still it is encouraging how many greet them with a smile, accepting the invitation with enthusiasm.

"It's about time someone did something like this!" many of them say.

"Grilled fish…how unique…we'd be glad to come," say many others.

They ask questions.

"Should I bring a side dish?"

"Do you want me to bring a dessert?"

"If I bring iced tea, would six gallons be enough?"

"Does green salad go with fish?"

"Can we bring the children?"

"Yes…yes…yes…" George and Martha say to all of their questions.

When they first started out, George and Martha only assumed Jesus would be doing most if not all the talking. Interesting enough, Jesus says little, leaving them to do most of the talking. At first, they find it a bit awkward to speak to strangers; although after a house or two, they find it becomes easy and downright fun. Oddly enough, there are four homes where Jesus takes the lead.

Thirteen

Leo and Dianne

Dianne insisted Leo wear his uniform at their wedding. He looked so handsome in it; she was so proud of him. Not only was she proud of him for his service to his country, but also for his service to his God. He is an upright, Churchgoing, God-fearing man who she not only loves but respects – holding him in high esteem.

In fact, it was at church they met. They both attended the same adult Sunday Bible class. It was not unusual for Leo to be called on to teach the class when the main teacher was unable to be there. Leo possessed a clear understanding of his faith and the Bible; and all agreed someday he would be a fine apologetic – a true defender of the faith.

He was polite and kind to her, although he was with everyone else at church. Dianne hoped for more than friendship, yet how could she make that happen. She made a fuss over him whenever possible. Still, Leo did not take the hint. Finally, in desperation Dianne took things into her own hands, asking Leo out on a date – dinner and a movie. That night changed everything. Leo finally got to see the real Dianne; he liked what he saw. As well, the evening proved to Dianne she was right about Leo all along.

From then on, they only dated each other. After ten months of courtship, Leo got down on one knee, proposing to Dianne. She said "yes" before the last word left his lips. Two months later, they married at the same church they met. They moved into a small apartment, furnishing it with a government loan. That was the one fly in the ointment of Dianne's plans. Once they were engaged, Leo enlisted in the army. He figured it was instant employment with good benefits for his wife and him and any children that may come later. As well as an instant small loan to get started in their life together.

Dianne wasn't happy about Leo's choice. All that time they'd be separated was not what she was wanting. Yet, she never voiced her disapproval. Besides, it was too late. It was something destined to happen whether she liked it or not. She'd just make the best of it. After all, it wouldn't be forever.

Leo being away for weeks at boot came was hard on Dianne; still that was only the beginning of her hardships.

During the Gulf War, Leo found himself shipped to the Middle East. Dianne prayed everyday for his safe return. A week didn't go by in which she didn't receive a letter from her husband. She always wrote him back in kind.

One day the letters just stopped coming. This worried Dianne to no end. Was he somewhere unable to write? Was he hurt – wounded – or God forbid, worse? She made inquires to the military. After weeks, she received a letter from his Commanding Officer assuring her Leo was well. In the letter he mentioned he spoke with Leo concerning his not writing his wife. Leo declined to comment on the matter, only to say he refused to write any letters home – to his wife or to anyone else for that matter.

It confused Dianne. Why would he not write? Still, this did not deter Dianne from writing to him. She wrote a letter nearly everyday, telling how much she loved him, begging him to write back. Yet no letters arrived.

Finally, when his tour of duty ended, she met him at the airport. She ran to him, falling into his arms. He held her tightly, kissed her, telling her how much he missed and loved her. This relinquished all the anguish she carried over the long months waiting for his return – wondering if she'd lost him – she hadn't.

Back in their small apartment, Dianne did her best to make him feel at home. Everything was neat as a pin; she'd prepared all his favorite dishes for that evening dinner. Inwardly, she held so many questions. Still, she bided her time, waiting for the right moment.

Over dinner, when all was calm, she asked why he'd stopped writing.

He looked at her with great sorrow in his eyes. "I'm not the man I was, Dianne. I've sinned…sinned past all forgiveness." She sat back in her chair, staring at him. He continued, "Oh, don't think it was another woman, because it wasn't. Only I wish it was. A sin like that can be easily forgiven and forgotten. No, my sins are much greater." Beyond that, he spoke not a word of his exploits. From that day on he never read his Bible nor stepped into a Church, again.

Now years later, their marriage was a good one. They were blessed with a fine home and a good life. He stayed true to his vows, remaining loyal and loving to Dianne. They never found cause to argue except on matters of religion. To keep the peace, she said little about such things. There was only one thing left to do; that was to pray for him – the man she loved.

****

"Who is it, dear?" Dianne calls out from the kitchen.

Leo stands at the open front door, never taking his eyes off Jesus, George and Martha. "Some of the neighbors from down the block. They want to invite us to a cookout at their place, tonight."

"Well, don't just leave them standing in the doorway; invite them in," says Dianne, wiping her hands dry as she steps out of the kitchen.

"Dianne says you can come in." Leo opens the door wide.

"You'll have to forgive my husband. Leo is not what you call the social type."
Dianne's smile is large and genuine.

"So, what's this about a cookout at your place?"

"Just that," Martha responds, "a backyard cookout for the neighborhood."

"Sounds like fun," says Dianne. "What should we bring?"

"Any side dish that goes with grilled fish."

"Grilled fish?" laughs Dianne. "Now that's different."

"Give…me…a…break," Leo declares. He rolls his eyes, staring at the ceiling. "What are you people selling?"

"Selling?" George asks.

"Yeah…selling; everybody's got an angle; what's yours? We go to your get-together, eat the free food, and the next thing you know we're looking at brochures of vacation time-shares in Boca Rattan."

"We're not selling anything!" George demands. "We just thought inviting our neighbors to a cookout would be a friendly, Christian, thing to do."

"There's the keyword…Christian," declares Leo. "What are you with one of those weirdo churches, selling salvation at a dollar a pound?"

Jesus walks forward and stands directly in front of Leo. He takes Leo aside, whispering so none of the others can hear them.

"What are you afraid of, Leo?"

"Afraid…I'm not scared of anything!"

"Oh, yes you are. You've run scared all your life and now more than ever. What is it you're afraid of?" Jesus asks. "You're afraid their message of salvation might make sense?"

"Salvation…? There's no such thing; and if there was, what makes you think it's for me?"

"If there's no such thing, you have nothing to fear, Leo," Jesus response. "If you're not afraid, just come, eat the free fish and then go home."

"I just might do that," says Leo.

It's not the first time Leo embarrassed Dianne; she's grown used to making excuses for him.

"Like I said, Leo's not what you call the social type. Thanks for the invite; only I don't think we can make it."

"We'll be there," Leo proclaims.

"I guess we'll be there," says Dianne, smiling, sounding confused.

"Six o'clock," Martha smiles.

Fourteen

Cameron and Vanessa

Cameron was an only child, well cared for and loved. His parents were good people; they tried to instill the *Golden Rule* into his life from an early age. *Do unto others as you would have them do unto you* worked well for them. Most people would consider them moral and upright, as they also felt they were.

They were not churchgoing people. They didn't have anything against religion, per say, only what was the point? Goodness can be found in everyone, if they're willing to work at it – Conscious Discipline. Within everyone is the understanding of right and wrong, good and evil. All it takes is the decision to follow that path and the effort to stay on it.

With all due respect to his parents, though he truly believed in their philosophy of life, it still wasn't enough. There had to be something else. As soon as Cameron was old enough, he began to investigate, studying every religion and reading their holy books. This didn't get him closer. Most of it didn't make much sense to him. Still, the bases of all religions seemed to be the same, *Do onto others as you would have them do to you*, which lined up with what his parents already taught him.

Believing he'd gotten all he could from his seeking, he began to look to science and philosophy. After reading hundreds of books on the subject, it was clear there was a connection between religion, science, and philosophy. Somehow it all linked, but how? It became his life's quest to find the answer.

During his college years, Cameron became interested in Yoga. A local Yoga teacher offered a one-night free class in the school gym. Cameron took the class and was immediately hooked. He began reading all the books on Yoga he could get his hands on. He not only filled his days with Yoga classes he studied the philosophy that accompanied it. Finally, he'd found the connection he'd been looking for. Everything he'd learned from his parents plus everything he'd learned on his own meld into one idea. His life finally had purpose and direction.

Straight out of college, Cameron landed a primo job with the firm of Williams and Williams. Surprisingly, they not only agreed to his asking salary, but to his demands for four weeks vacation a year; two of which taken simultaneously every summer. Being now a devout follower of the path of Yoga, he would never think of missing the Summer Solstice Yoga Retreat. Every solstice in the wilds of New Mexico – for two weeks and he didn't want to miss a day.

The fifth summer he attended he flew into Flagstaff, Arizona, rented a car and drove to the campsite. It felt great to see all his old friends he'd made over the last few years. His cabin partner that year was Doug Silverman, a Yoga teacher from Ontario. This was not a strange occurrence as people from all over the world flocked to New Mexico for the two-week retreat.

The days were filled with Yoga classes, meditation, health food classes, and the like. There was also plenty of time for socializing and fun: softball, volleyball, sing-a-longs, and dances in the evening after supper. It was at one of these dances that Cameron's life changed.

She was a blonde haired beauty who caught his eye unlike no other woman. From a friend of a friend he learned her name – Vanessa. She was an only child raised in San Francisco by her parents who'd once been flower children. Even later, much of their philosophy of life remained with them. As with all parents, they raised Vanessa by their standards and values. Unlike Cameron, a Yoga retreat was nothing new. It was just a continuation of the way she was raised – the path she'd always known.

Thoughts of her hounded him all-day, everyday of the retreat. He dreamed of her every night. Her face was always before him. It haunted him till even during his meditations many were the times he forgot his Mantra. The only sound echoing in his mind – Vanessa…Vanessa…Vanessa.

He hadn't gone unnoticed by her, either. From the moment she laid eyes on him, she thought of nothing else. She learned from a friend of a friend his name was Cameron.

It was during a late night pizza party at the camp (heavy on the veggies, no meat or cheese, of course) he got up his nerve to approach her, introducing himself to her. They talked for hours, amazed how much they had in common and how much they though alike.

"I just love Yoga, don't you?" she asked him.

"Definitely."

"It's such a perfect fit. You see, I'm a very spiritual being, not religious, mind you, just very spiritual."

"Yeah, me too."

The rest is romantic history.

They felt overjoyed to find out they not only came from the same state but they lived a mere ten miles from each other. Surely, this was kismet.

Back home, two weeks later, they dated every chance they had. Six weeks after that, they rented a house and moved in together.

One year later, just after a meditation session together, as Vanessa put out the sandalwood incense, she asked Cameron a life changing question.

"Cam, why don't we get married?" she whispered.

"Married…?" he asked, shocked she would ask such a thing. He always felt they were equally yoked; and such things were nonsense.

"It's not for me. I hope you know that." she said. "It's just that it would get my mother off my back."

"I though your mother was a freethinker?"

"She is…except when it comes to her daughter."

"It's just a piece of paper!" Cameron protested.

"Well, then, if it's just a piece of paper, what harm is there in getting married?"

This was a logic he could find no fault in.

"Okay...but it's got to be a Justice of the Peace. None of that Holy, Holy stuff your grandmother's into."

After five years of wedded bliss, Cameron and Vanessa were still very much in love. Many were the times in bed late at night, he would whisper to her. "I hope after we die, and reincarnate, we come back as husband and wife."

"Yeah, except next time you can come back as the woman, and I'll come back as the man," she would say. They both laughed at that.

****

"Come in, come in, please." Cameron and Vanessa couldn't have been friendlier, eagerly opening their home to the three strangers.

The entire house decorated in a Far-Eastern motif. There are fine tapestries on the walls as well as the floors, furniture is sparse and low to the floor, dozens of lit candles are about the house; there is a strong smell of recently burned incense.

"A cookout, what a great way to create a sense of community...a sense of oneness throughout the neighborhood; I'm all for it. I think it's great!" Vanessa announces with excitement. "Only, Cameron and I don't eat fish; we're strict vegans. If it's all the same to you, we can bring our own food. Don't worry, it won't be anything too weird; we'll bring enough to share with others," she says laughing.

"Vegan...is that for health reasons?" Martha asks.

"Partially...but mostly because of our beliefs; you see, we believe everything has a soul, even rocks and trees."

"What are your beliefs?" Jesus asks.

"Enlightenment, my friend," says Cameron. "Come, I'll show you."

He guides them to a small table where sit a half dozen framed portraits, each with a lit candle before it.

"This is a photo of Swami Baba; we visit him in India every chance we get. He is beyond doubt an *Enlightened Being*; you can feel the energy coming from him just by being in his presence."

"Who are these others?"

"This is Buddha. Did you know the name Buddha means Enlightened One? And this is Vishnu and Krishna...all Enlightened Beings."

"Who is this one here? He looks familiar," Jesus asks, pointing to the last frame.

"That is Jesus Christ," Cameron states with resolve.

"Was he an Enlightened Being, too?"

"Most definitely; through sacrifice, suffering, many reincarnations, and deep mediation, he was able to realize the god within…the god within us all that someday we will realize; in short, Enlightenment!"

"I see," Jesus says.

Cameron burst into laughter. "I'm sure this all sounds crazy to you; it did to me at first; me coming from a middle-class background and all. It's hard for the westerner to get his mind around many of these ideas. You probably think I'm an incredible fool."

"No, I don't think you're a fool," Jesus responds. "I think you're a spiritual person who's done the best he can on his own." Jesus points to George, "You know, George, here, is a spiritual person, too. The two of you should get together sometime and compare notes."

"I'd like that," Cameron says, smiling.

George's eyes go wide, as if someone hollered to him, "Here catch", and tossed him a live snake. "Who…me?" George asks, nervously.

"Don't be so modest, George," Jesus says. "You have a lot to share with others."

"We best get going," Martha declares. "We'll see you two tonight around six o'clock."

Outside, George looks forlorn. *What do I have to share with others?* he thinks.

Jesus reaches out to him, holding his arm as they walk together.

"You know, George, there are many differences between a believer and a nonbeliever. One: is the nonbeliever can only see the world through his own limited eyes. Believers have the Holy Spirit to guide and guard them. The life of the believer is the only life that comes with a guarantee and owner's manual."

"An owner's manual?" George asks.

"Yes, an owner's manual. It's called the Bible, George. Everything you need to know on this planet now is in that book. All you need do is to read it."

Fifteen

Tommy and Trish

Gregory Milton was a self-made man, and proud of it. He started the Milton Foundry on a shoestring, turning it into a multimillion dollar company. The work was hard and long, yet to him well worth it. There's an old saying: *In a foundry something is either heavy, sharp, or scalding hot; but most often it's all three.*

He was also proud of his long-lasting marriage to his wife, Gabriella, a dark haired Italian beauty he fell in love with when he was stationed in Europe. Even now, twenty-five years later her beauty hadn't faded. He beamed with pride whenever he walked into a restaurant or a party with Gabriella on his arm. You felt the breeze from all the men's heads turning just to get a look at her.

Above all this, the pinnacle of his life's joy was his daughter, Trish. He loved, cherished, protected, and spoiled her in every way, shape and form a father can think of.

All her life she could and did no wrong in his eyes. She truly was *Daddy's little girl* or "My little Princess", as he liked to call her.

On her eighteenth birthday – the age of consent – the age of womanhood – the age a young person can do as they please – she unintentionally broke her father's heart.

She announced to her parents and to the whole world her love for Tommy Galloway – a young welder who worked at her father's foundry. Greg Milton liked and respected the young man; he was a good worker – honest and mature. But he was from the streets – unschooled and uncouth – certainly not worthy of his one and only child.

Greg Milton grew up on the streets. He understood the kind of man Tommy was. He knew that for all Tommy's good qualities, he'd always be a low-class loser. Of course, Milton worked his way out of that life, however he was the exception. Sure, possibly Tommy could be too, but that was a chance he feared taking. He tried putting his foot down, but this only placed him and his daughter at a distance from each other. He also considered firing Tommy, except he knew that would make Trish turn against him. Still, he spoke against the romance whenever he could, vowing to fight it at every turn.

Gabriella saw things different from her husband. She always prayed for the best for her daughter. Tommy was not rich in money; still his other qualities were far better than a rich man who couldn't make her daughter happy. And her daughter's happiness was always foremost. She understood wealth isn't a guarantee for happiness. She'd seen what it did to her husband. She knew love is love and far better than anything a person can offer another.

Trish and her parents argued through the night and into the morning. At which point, Trish realized for the first time in her life her father would not agree to her wants and needs. He would never change his mind, she knew that. Rushing upstairs to her room, in tears she packed her bags to leave home.

At the front door, Gabriella blocked the way out.

"Mother, I've got to go," said Trish. "I love him."

As much as she didn't want her daughter to leave, she hadn't a good argument to *I love him*. All she could think was Trish was as stubborn as her father. She moved aside.

Trish opened the door. Gabriella stood in the doorway with tears in her eyes, pleading with both her daughter and her husband not be so rash, to continue talking until they could find a solution.

Greg remained seated in the large armchair in the parlor. The back of the armchair was turned to the front door. He held a snifter of brandy, sipping ever so slowly, ignoring the protest of his daughter and pleading of his wife.

The next instant, without closing the door behind her, Trish ran to the street where Tommy sat in his car waiting for her.

Gabriella stood hopelessly watching Trish tossing her things in the backseat of his car, and then driving off.

Greg rose from his armchair, still holding his brandy; he gently moved his wife from the doorway, slamming the door closed. He looked at her sternly, speaking coldly, "From here on out, I have no daughter; and I forbid you to see her or to speak her name, again."

It is a sorrowful fact that pride is a two-edged sword.

****

Martha is just about to press the doorbell when loud noises coming from within stop her. It's clear a man and woman are inside having a squabble. What they are saying is not clear; yet a few of the shouted statements are audible. Something about someone doesn't listen, someone doesn't care; someone is too selfish to love.

Embarrassed, Martha backs from the door. "Seems we've come at a bad time; maybe, we should skip this one."

"No…let's continue," Jesus says, knocking on the door. "I know a cry for help when I hear one."

The quarreling stops for a moment only to start again louder than before.

"Where do you think you're going?"

"There's someone at the door!"

"Forget the door, come back here!"

The door opens revealing an obviously pregnant young woman.

"Yes, can I help you?" she asks.

A second later, a young man appears at her side.

"Can I help you folks?" he asks, sounding belligerent.

"Yes, we're from the neighborhood, we're having a backyard cookout later today, and we'd like to invite you and your wife."

"She's not my wife; she's my girlfriend. And I don't think now is a good time for this."

"I'm sorry if we've come at a bad time," Jesus says. "We'd like you to come this evening around six. This is George and Martha, my name is Jesus. What are your names?"

"Listen buddy, I told you, now is not a good time for this."

"My name is Trish and this is Tommy," the young woman burst out despite her boyfriends objections.

"Listen, I told you this is a bad time," says Tommy. "Thanks for the invite; but I don't think we'll be making it."

Martha takes out a small pad and pen from her pocket, writing down their address, handing it to Trish. "Here, this is our address. We live just up the street.

"If you and your wife change your minds, it starts at six," George adds.

"I told you, she's not my wife. Now if you don't mind!" says Tommy, slamming the door. Within, the argument continues.

"What a shame," Martha murmurs softly, just loud enough for the other two to hear.

Jesus turns, walking toward the street. "Don't worry, they'll be there," He says.

Sixteen

Patricia

Patricia was the youngest of six children, raised in the Midwest on her parents' farm. They raised their children on whole milk, greens, fresh eggs, fried chicken, and the Good Book. They were hardworking, simple people, proud people, good people, and churchgoing folk.

Patricia's faith was strong even from a young age. Accepting the gift of Christ was as natural as breathing. She was saved at the age of six. She would have sooner, only her parents wanted her to be old enough to fully understand what she believed. On the Sunday she was baptized, her father was so joyful and proud he took the family to town for lunch at the restaurant in the Parker House Hotel. This wasn't something they did often, perhaps every five years. That's how important it was to them.

As she grew into womanhood, everyone at her Church looked up to Patricia as a shining example.

"No mountain is too high to climb, no river too wide…with Jesus," she would say. She was not a fair-weather Christian. When misfortune would strike, she budged not an inch. When others were hurting, she was the first to listen, and the last to leave.

Knowing this, it seemed only fitting she married Dell, an up-and-coming young man in the church. Most folks knew someday he would be an elder – it was only his age preventing him at that point.

Patricia and Dell knew each other since grade school. It wasn't till high school either one took notice of the other. The attraction was strong. They dated until graduation. Dell was off to college; Patricia remained living with her parents, working at the five-and-ten in town. Dell promised to return someday to marry Patricia. As much as she wanted it to be so, Patricia put little hope into it, figuring it was just a young man dizzy from romance.

However, Dell did come back. He set up an insurance office in town. He did well, after all he was a local boy and people trusted him. The first thing he did on the day he returned was to march up to Patricia's father and ask for her hand in marriage.

"She's yours, if she'll have you," her father said.

Patricia overheard from the kitchen, she rushed into the parlor where they were, proclaiming "Yes" before Dell could pop the question. In fact, it was a week into their engagement they realized he never did propose. Wanting to do things proper, one night Dell got down on one knee and asked her.

When Patricia and Dell married, nearly the entire congregation attended the wedding. Patricia's family took up an entire pew in the church, all dressed in their Sunday best. Arm in arm, her father walked her down the aisle, as her mother cried. Dell stood at the altar waiting, looking as happy as a man can be.

It was a pot-luck affair, everyone bringing something. Not having enough money to feed everyone was well understood in the community; no one looked down on them. Friends and family filled the Church hall to capacity for the reception; there was singing and joy late into the night.

They honeymooned at the Parker House for the weekend. It was all they could afford both moneywise and time away from work.

The couple rented a modest little home in a modest little neighborhood – walking distance to their jobs and the church. As with many young couples they were unable to afford a car.

Singularly, each had been an example to all at the Church; but as a couple they exceeded every expectation. Everyone knew and loved Patricia and Dell.

Two months before their first wedding anniversary, Patricia announced she was pregnant. They knew it would be difficult, they had such little money; still they knew with God's help they would be fine.

It was in the eight month of her pregnancy, Mitchell, an old college pal of Dell, came for a visit. He drove up their driveway on a motorcycle that roared so loud it shook the entire neighborhood. Mitchell was the freewheeling type; all he owned he'd tied to the back of his bike. A bit unorthodox, but after a few hours of talking with him, Patricia liked him almost as much as Dell did.

On the third day of his visit, he offered Patricia a ride on his bike. Dell was against it at first; she being in the condition she was.

"Dell, don't worry," laughed Mitchell. "I'll drive like an old man; she can wear my helmet. Besides, if she falls off she'd only bounce." He pointed to her oversized stomach. They all laughed; and Dell gave his permission.

Patricia held on tight to Mitchell as they whizzed up and down the town's main street. At the corner of sixth and Washington, the light turned from green to amber. To make the light, Mitchell sped up; they didn't make it. A driver, seeing the cycle and not knowing what he should do, hit his breaks, stopping dead center in the intersection. The cycle smashed into the side of the car. Mitchell hit the roof of the car and was instantly killed. Patricia flew twenty feet over the car, landing headfirst in the street.

At the hospital, the doctors told Dell the x-rays showed the baby to be fine; although there was no guarantee. As for his wife, she was in a coma; she might remain there one day, one year, five days, fifty years, there was no way of telling. As for her mental and physical health when or if she ever emerged from the coma, that too came with no guarantee.

Weeks went by, the Church, the community stood beside Dell in his plight. But none stood as close as Monica, Patricia's now widowed mother. Her father died just months after her and Dell's wedding. The hard life of a farmer eventually wore him down. Patricia's mother remained at the hospital by Dell's side, night and day. Often the two would fall to their knees and pray. Monica was as strong a Christian as her daughter, and a comfort to Dell.

The doctors took Dell aside, telling him the time had come for the birth of his child.

"Can you do that...I mean in her condition?" he asked.

"With a cesarean and your permission...we can."

Dell gave his permission. That night, he and Monica waited alone in the waiting room for word of the birth of his child.

With tears in his eyes, Dell turned to Monica. "I can't do this, Mom...I just can't. It's all too much! What if there's something wrong with the baby? What if Patricia never comes out of the coma? What if she comes out and she's an invalid? I can't do this, Mom...I just can't!"

"Dell, listen to me; I know this is hard on you; but with God's help..."

"I can't do this, Monica!" He jumped from his seat and ran out the door. "Tell Patricia I'm sorry!" were his last words. No one in town or at Church ever heard from or about Dell again – ever.

The child born was a girl. Monica named it Jenny, after her mother, Patricia's grandmother – she figured Patricia would have liked that.

Eventually, they moved the unconscious Patricia and young Jenny to the family farm. Thankfully, all her siblings were grown and moved away. This meant there was more than enough room for mother and child. It also meant they could not expect help from family members. It was a full-time, difficult job taking care of Patricia and the baby. Though friends often came to help out, it was a hard life for Monica.

After months of prayer by the entire church, Patricia came out of her coma; but she was not well. She would have to learn to walk and speak again. Patricia worked hard at her recovery. Her faith and her incentive was a help to her. She wanted to be able to hold Jenny, so she worked her upper muscles. She wanted to walk with her child, so she struggled to walk again. She dreamed of telling Jenny she loved her. She didn't want her child raised by anyone other than her, so she struggled – prayed and struggled.

"Besides, I don't want my own eight-month-old daughter showing me up," Patricia once said, laughingly, in her still slurred speech, of her child who was showing signs of speaking and walking.

After three years of intense therapy, Patricia was as close to normal as any of the doctors could hope for. Finally, she was able to take care of her Jenny. When Patricia was well enough – as if by some unwritten law – Monica died in her sleep.

"Grandma's gone to be with Jesus," she told Jenny.

Patricia received a job at the Church. It wasn't a good job, but it paid enough to keep her and her daughter alive. In fact, the entire Church helped whenever possible – Patricia was grateful.

Just after Jenny's fourth birthday, Patricia took her to the doctor for her biannual check up. They found something. What? Don't know; we'll do some tests. What? Still don't know; we'll do some more tests. What? What? What? It's leukemia.

Patricia was a prayer warrior to begin with; yet nothing compared with the praying she did for her Jenny. Still, for all her prays, for all her fasting and pleading with God, it was no use. Jenny died quietly in her mother's arms.

****

"I guess we've knocked on every door in the neighborhood," Martha reports.

"All but one..." Jesus says, pointing to an upstairs garage apartment behind one of the larger houses.

"Gee, I never noticed that was there," Martha says.

"That's just what she was hoping." Jesus turns to face George. "It's getting late. George, you need to go get the fish. Don't look in your wallet now but there's some extra money in it. I want you to go to the Butcher Shop and use the money to buy the fish."

"But the Butcher Shop only sells meat and poultry; he doesn't sell fish," George says.

"He will today. I want you to walk in and say to the Butcher, 'The Master wants fish'. He'll have plenty for you at a good price. You best go now; Martha and I will invite this last neighbor."

Without another word, George turns and walks off, while Jesus and Martha make their way up the wooden staircase to the garage apartment.

Only a screened door covers the entrance; Jesus knocks gently on it. No sound comes from inside; Jesus knocks again.

"Go away," a voice calls from the darkness inside.

Jesus speaks through the screen, "Patricia, open the door, it's me."

"I know it's you and I don't care. Now go away!"

"Patricia, please; I need to speak with you."

A moment passes; someone pushes the screened door slightly ajar; a small, sad looking woman stands in the opening.

"Don't you ever give up," she says, looking unswervingly at the face of Jesus.

"Would you really want me to?" He asks.

She turns and goes back inside. "You might as well come in; you're going to do what you want anyway; I can't stop you."

Inside, it amazed Martha how unkempt the apartment is. In college, she had seen apartments of young bachelors look almost as bad, but nothing like this, especially by a woman – a grown woman. A mountain of dirty dishes looms in the kitchen sink and on the small dinner table. Dirty clothes sprawled everywhere – over chairs, the coffee table, and on the floor. Unwashed cups and glasses rest on top of nearly every flat surface; and empty wine bottles litter the entire apartment.

Patricia grabs the closest empty wineglass; taking a half empty bottle, pours herself a drink.

"You want a drink?" She holds out the glass to her two guests. Jesus shakes his head. She continues to rave, "No, of course you don't want any…not with me you don't. Say, wasn't wine one of your specialties? Is it still your blood if it's a cheap skid row white? And what about that *changing water into wine* trick of yours? If you really want to help a gal, that's some hocus-pocus I could make good use of."

It's clear from the slur of her words she's drunk. She staggers over to Martha.

"Did He tell you anything about me?"

"No…" Martha whispers, shaking her head.

"Did He tell you how He let me fall in love with Him when I was a young girl and how He promised to always stand by me through thick and thin? Oh, and He did, for awhile! When things got crazy and all my nonbeliever and believing friends made fun of me and refused to have anything to do with me and I hadn't a friend in the world, He stood by me. When I became pregnant and the man I loved turned his back on me and refused me and my child, He stood by me. When I was nine months pregnant and thrown into a coma, He stood by me. When I became the gossip of the entire town, He stood by me."

With tears in her eyes, she looks straight at Jesus.

"But when I needed Him the most, he was nowhere to be found!"

Jesus looks sorrowfully back at her.

"I was always there for you," He says gently.

"Like hell you were!" she shouts back at Him, hurling the glass of wine, it shatters to pieces at His feet. "Jenny meant everything to me; she was my whole world! I held my four-year-old daughter in my arms and I prayed to you; and you let her die!"

Patricia bursts into weeping so strong she cannot continue.

As if in a dream, by some strange impulse, Martha reaches out placing her hand on Patricia's shoulder.

"I'm having a cookout at my home, this evening at six. It'd mean a lot to me if you came," Martha says in a low voice, not sure if it is the right thing to say, not sure if Patricia hears a word of it.

Martha turns and walks out, followed by Jesus. At the door, He turns to face Patricia one more time. He's about to speak but she stops Him.

"Don't say it…I know…you love me! Well, it doesn't mean a thing to me now; because…I…don't…love…you!"

Martha watches Jesus slowly descend the wooden staircase. She sees how sorrowful he feels. She wants to say something, except she finds no words.

Jesus wept.

Seventeen

The Butcher Shop

Dan stands at the back door of his Butcher Shop, eating a sandwich as he watches the delivery truck back up to the building. Jeff, the truck driver, can see Dan in his side mirror, directing him.

"That's right, keep coming…keep coming," Dan shouts, waving his hand for Jeff to keep slowly coming back toward the building. Dan holds his palm up, shouting, "Stop…stop…you got it."

The writing on the side of the truck reads, *Davis and Davis Foods*. Jeff hops out the truck cab, holding a clipboard; he hands it to Dan.

The two men perform the usual greeting ceremony they have carried out every Saturday afternoon for the past ten years. Jeff opens the back of the truck, pulls out a ramp, and hops up. He piles boxes onto a handcart and wheels them down the ramp and into the shop, followed by Dan.

"Now, let's see," says Jeff as he takes the boxes off the handcart one by one and places them on the floor. "Two boxes of Italian sausage…one hot, one mild."

Dan examines the order form on the clipboard; he finds the two boxes. He echoes the order back to Jim so each can agree on the order, "Two Italian sausages…one hot, one mild…check."

Jeff continues taking boxes off the cart. "That's one case of *London Pub Steak Sauce* and one case of *Billy Red's Memphis Style Barbecue Rub*."

Dan runs his pencil up and down the list till he finds the two cases.

"Sauce…rub…check."

Jeff places the last case on the floor. "And one case of fresh Tilapia packed in ice."

"Whoa…whoa!" bellows Dan. "Tilapia, that's fish!"

"Yeah, so…? You ordered it!" says Jeff, pointing to his order form.

"There's got to be some mistake," Dan complains. He looks Jeff square in the eye, "Jeff, you've been making deliveries here for how many years…ten? In all those ten years, when have I ordered fish?"

"Hey, don't ask me. I just do what I'm told and you've got Tilapia on your order."

Dan eyes the order form once more; sure enough, there's the Tilapia.

Jeff points to the case on the floor. "They had this fish flown in early this morning packed in ice. There isn't a piece of fish in the state as fresh as these, unless you caught it yourself out at Lake Whitney early this morning. Why don't you put it out and see how your costumers feel about it. Tilapia…it's a great fish for grilling."

"Wait here," Dan orders Jeff. He goes to his office, picks up the phone and dials.

"You've reached Davis and Davis Foods, the finest in food products. We're sorry, but due to the large volume of calls your waiting time is estimated to be fifteen minutes," announces a sweet, singsong, female voice on the other end of the line. "If you press one now on your phone dial, you can leave your name and number. We will contact you as soon as possible. Again, we are sorry for the inconvenience. Thank you for shopping Davis and Davis."

Dan hangs up and marches out of his office, back to the loading dock, right up to Jeff.

"Listen, Jeff," says Dan, pushing the clipboard into Jeff's gut, "this is a butcher shop, right? We sell Beef, chicken, pork, turkey during the Holidays, and wild game when someone orders it special. But never have we sold, or will we ever sell, any fish!"

"Okay, I get it," responds Jeff. "I'll just put it back on the truck. Shame though, it's the freshest around. Oh, when you get the bill, pay it, but send a letter with the payment telling them what happened and they'll refund your money."

"When will I get my refund?"

"In thirty days."

"Thirty days...you've got to be kidding?"

"Would I kid you?"

Just then, the bell over the front door rings out – it's George. Dan rushed out from the back to the front of the shop followed by Jeff. Dan's mood changes immediately from grumpy to friendly. Martha and George usually buy their meat and poultry at the supermarket. Dan doesn't recognize George as a regular customer, so he goes out of his way to be extra friendly.

"Good day to you, sir," says Dan, smiling. "How can I help you, today?"

George bends low, looking into the glass casing. He sees the usual: beef, pork, and chicken. There's nothing that looks remotely like fish. He shakes his head, walking over to the counter. He knows word for word what he's supposed to say; he rehearsed it in his head during the entire ride to the Butcher Shop. But now, standing in front of two men staring and smiling at him, he feels uncomfortable saying it. Finally, he closes his eyes, blurting it out.

"The Master says...the Master says He wants fish!" George opens his eyes to see the two men's reaction. There is none; they are still smiling.

Then, what they just heard sinks in. Some of the smile leaves Dan's face. He turns to give Jeff a look of excitement. A look that says: *Did you just hear what I just heard?*

Jeff's smile disappears completely. His eyebrows rise high. He shoots a look at Dan that says: *Don't look at me, I just deliver the stuff.*

Dan turns back to George with only half a smile and hopefulness in his voice, "Fish...did you say, fish?"

George could easily answer *yes*, but he rehearsed what to say during the drive to the shop. He fells proud he found the courage to say it out loud. Such courage deserves commending and repeating. So, George takes in a deep breath and lets it out, again, "The Master says He wants fish!"

Dan couldn't believe his ears. The full smile returns to his face. "Fish...? Yes, of course!" Dan proclaims gladly. "I have some lovely Tilapia on ice, flown in fresh this morning. It's on special today; I can give it to you for cost. Tilapia...it's a great fish for grilling."

George takes out his wallet, examining the contents. There is a hundred dollar bill he is sure was not there before.

"How much will you give me for one-hundred dollars?"

Dan looks at the order form in Jeff's hands; the price of the twenty-five pounds of fresh fish is slightly more than one-hundred dollars. He doesn't want to argue anymore with Jeff and he doesn't want to go through any red tape with Davis and Davis Foods; he just wants the case of Tilapia out of there and forgotten.

"I can give you twenty-five pounds!"

"Fine, I'll take it," George says.

"Very good, sir," says Dan. "I'll just have Jeff here help you take it out to your car for you."

Jeff uses his handcart to take up the box of Tilapia, following George. Before going out the door, Jeff shrugs his shoulders toward Dan who can only shrug his shoulders back. Both of them are in confused disbelief.

When the bell over the door rings, the thought finally comes into Dan's mind clearly. *Master...master, what the heck was that guy talking about?*

Eighteen

The Cookout

Like the Magi bearing gifts, at six o'clock, invited households begin entering George and Martha's backyard.

There are four green bean casseroles, two green salads, six gallons of iced tea, a cooler of soda pop, various vegetable dishes, plastic bowls filled with onion dip and chips for dipping. For dessert there's chocolate cake, a box of donuts, and a plate of homemade oatmeal cookies.

George is at the grill keeping a close eye on the fish. Martha sets places at the picnic table and two card tables she setup for the overspill. Many of the guests bring folding chairs, placing them about the yard. A young teenage boy plays his guitar; music fills the air. Children run about playing tag. Shouts of "you're it...you're it" blend with the music. Some of the women help Martha set the tables while the men stand around questioning one another what each does for a living. The atmosphere is good.

"So, what did our vegan friends bring?" Jesus whispers in Martha's ear.

She whispers in His ear, "Babylonian Layered Surprise."

He backs from her just enough to look her squarely in the eye. For a moment there is a blank stare on his face; then suddenly, his entire body erupts with laughter.

"It is all right to joke with you?" Martha asks. "I mean, I haven't done anything wrong?"

Still laughing, he pulls her near and hugs her. "Martha...you are so precious to me"

George places a large platter of cooked fish in the center of the main table. There are grill-marks on the fillets. A savory aroma fills the air. Everyone is surprised. Never thinking about grilling fish for a picnic, at that moment, it seems like the best thing anyone can think of eating.

"Fish is ready!" he announces. "Come and get it! Everyone, find yourselves a seat! Fish is ready!"

"Did everyone make it?" Jesus asks, looking at the small crowd.

"Just about," Martha says. "Everyone but that young couple who was arguing; and I'm sorry to say, that poor woman from the garage apartment."

"You mean Patricia?" Jesus says. "No, she's here."

Martha turns to look in the same direction Jesus is looking. Patricia is standing at the backyard gate. She appears sober. Her look is neat, her disposition calm yet distant; she enters.

Jesus takes his place next the head of the table across from Martha.

"Lord..." George whispers to Jesus, "It is right that you sit at the head of the table."

"No, George, you are the head of this household, it's your place."

"Then at least say grace and bless the food for us," George insists.

"No, George, as I said, you are the head of this household; and with that position come great responsibilities; one of which is to pray over the food."

George stands at the head of the table.

"Ladies and Gentlemen…neighbors…if we could be quiet for a moment, we'd like to give thanks."

It takes a moment for parents to hush their children, getting them to stop for a minute. It's clear some feel awkward, not being the praying type. Yet it's something they all respect. Surprisingly, many of the guests gather in small circles, family members hugging family members with their heads bowed. George reaches out, taking Martha's hand in his. Without any prompting, one by one, each guest takes another's hand till the entire group is hand in hand.

George begins, "Heavenly Father, we praise your holy name. We thank you for this sweet day. We thank you for this food. We thank you for this gathering of neighbors and we ask you to bless every one of them. We ask you to bless this food towards nourishing our bodies that we may be instruments of your peace. We ask this all in the name of our savior, Jesus Christ, Amen."

Echoes of "Amen" make their way through the small group. They let go of one another's hands; laughter and conversation breakout as they take their seats, passing the food around.

The children naturally understand the card tables are for them. Patricia sits at one of the card tables farthest from Jesus; unexpectedly, feeling more comfortable with the children. The parents make up plates for their children, placing them before them. None of them look at all interested in eating.

One of the women makes up a plate for Patricia. She smiles at Patricia as she places the plate in front of her. Not wanting to be rude, Patricia offers a halfhearted smile and a whisper *"Thank You"*.

She keeps her eyes focused on her plate, afraid to look up; afraid to look on the face of Jesus, or worse, on the face of any of the children next to her. She moves the food about in her plate with her fork, not eating a bite.

The children pick at their food, eating little, more concerned with play, jumping out of their chairs after eating only a bite or two. They resume their loud, joyous romping throughout the yard. Patricia sits alone. A few other guests try to draw her into the conversation; she is polite, but has nothing to say.

Martha goes into the house to fetch more ice; the doorbell rings, she answers it. It's Trish, the pregnant young woman from earlier. She's holding a suitcase; she's crying.

"I'm sorry to intrude on you like this, only I didn't know where else to go."

"Don't even mention it; you're welcomed here. Come in, sweetheart," Martha says as she guides her in.

"Is everything all right?" Martha asks.

"I'll be fine in just a minute," says Trisha, sniffling, doing her best to hold back the tears.

"Has he hurt you?" Martha asks solemnly.

"Tommy...? No, Tommy would never hurt me. It's just that I can't...I can't..." She falls into Martha's arms, sobs uncontrollably.

"I just need to use your phone to call a cab. I'd have called from my house, but I didn't want Tommy to hear."

"There...there," whispers Martha, reaching for a tissue, dabbing it under Trish's eyes. "No need to call a cab; George can drive you anywhere you want to go. But first you need to get yourself together. Have you had anything to eat; are you hungry? There's still plenty of food outside. Let's get you freshened up and pretty again, and we'll get you something to eat." Martha guides her to the bedroom. Trish gazes into the mirror at her image. Her eyes are red and swollen. Martha hands her a face towel she run under hot water.

Outside, Trish sits at the main table; Martha makes up a dish, placing it in front of her. It's clear to the other guests she's been crying.

"You feel all right, honey?" Dianne asks, resting her hand on Trish's.

There's a tired look on Trish's face. She feels touched by the concern of those around her; she forces a smile. "I'm fine, thank you."

"How far along are you?" asks one of the other women.

"Oh, I've still got a couple of months left."

"Well, you go right ahead and eat and don't let us bother you."

Before she puts one bite of food in her mouth, she suddenly stops. Standing at the other end of the table is Tommy.

"Are you okay? I've been looking all over for you." There is true concern in Tommy's voice. "Do you want to come home?" he asks.

Trish stares at the plate of food before her, unable to look Tommy in the eye. "I was thinking I might go visit my mother."

"Go to your mother's...for how long?"

"I don't know, Tommy."

Everyone is silent; George whispers across the table, "If you two need some privacy, you're welcome to go inside."

"No, I want everyone to hear this," says Tommy as he approaches Trish.

"I know what this is about," he says to her. "I'm sorry, and I'm here to make things right."

He falls to his knees before her; taking a small box from his pocket he opens it, presenting her with a diamond engagement ring. He takes her hand.

"Trish, I love you and I want to spend the rest of my life with you. Will you marry me?"

She stares at the ring for a moment, looks to him and answers softly, "Yes, Tommy, I'll marry you."

He places the ring on her finger, reaches up and kisses her.

Everyone at the table watches silently; some of the women have tears running down their cheeks.

Tommy stands, taking her hand, again.

"Come on, I'll drive you to your mother's. Maybe we can go out for dinner tomorrow night and start making plans for the wedding?"

"It's a date," she says, standing up.

With his arm around her, they walk toward the gate opening.

"Wait…you forgot your luggage!" Martha runs to them, offering the suitcase; Tommy takes it.

"Thank you," he says to Martha. He turns to the other guests. "Thank you, all of you."

No one speaks until they are out of sight.

"That was so romantic! My Doug used to be romantic like that when we were young," a woman says, still wiping tears from her eyes.

"I still am…sorry if I haven't shown it lately," says Doug reaching over to his wife.

"Say, this is a party not a funeral; let's make some noise!" someone shouts.

"Noise…? That reminds me, where are the children?" asks another.

It's true; the background noise of children playing has stopped. They look around relieved to see Jesus sitting in a corner of the garden with the small group of children at his feet. It's obvious He is telling them stories; now and then they burst into laughter.

"I'll just see if He needs anything," George says, walking over to Jesus.

A small girl, no older than four, sitting on the grass closest to Jesus reaches out, placing her hand on the wound in his left foot.

"Do they hurt…all your holes…do they hurt?" she asks softly and with much concern.

"No, they don't hurt, anymore," Jesus says. "They hurt the day I got them; they don't hurt me, anymore."

"Like when someone gets their ears pierced so they can wear earrings!" proclaims a boy of six.

"Yes…something like that," Jesus responds.

"The children…the children can see you as you truly are?" George asks.

"Yes, of course," Jesus answers.

Again, George feels a twinge of shame and embarrassment. He knows too well there is a passage in the Bible about the *Little Children*; he can't remember it or even where it is in the Bible.

"Use your concordance, George; it makes looking things up so much easier," Jesus says as he rises from his chair. He smiles at the children. "Well, children, I do have to spend some time with the adults."

"No, tell us another story," they shout.

"I'll tell you what," He says. "I know someone who tells stories even better than I. Just wait, I'll go get her."

Jesus walks to the card table at the farthest end of the garden; right up to Patricia. Without a word, He takes her hand, guides her, and sits her down before the children.

"Children, this is Patricia, and Patricia tells the best stories and she just loves little children. So, listen carefully."

Patricia grabs the hand of Jesus, pressing it to her check. She looks to Him; her eyes are lonely, scared, and questioning.

"Don't worry," He whispers, "it will all be fine. I promise."

Sitting back at the main table, Jesus listens to the conversation. Not surprising, the topic turns to religion.

"Don't get me wrong, George" Cameron starts out saying, "I think the prayer you said before dinner was beautiful. Although it was clear from the words you used you're strictly Christian."

"And what's wrong with that?" Martha asks.

"Nothing, I think Jesus Christ is one of the best."

"*One* of the best...?" asks a guest sounding put off by the statement.

"See, that's just my point," says Cameron. "Christians get so defensive about their beliefs. Don't you think it's awfully closed-minded...this *One-Way* attitude?"

Some of the guests who are of the Christian persuasion try their best to state the facts, to defend their faith. But only one voice comes across as a true apologetic, a true champion for Christianity.

No, it isn't Jesus, neither is it George or Martha. To all's surprise, it's Leo. Even his wife, Dianne, looks awestruck.

"I can't make you believe Jesus Christ is the only way, but I can get you to understand what Christians mean when they say *One Way*," Leo says to Cameron. "When you hear the statement Jesus is the only way', what you do think?"

"Well, the first thing that comes to my mind is it's a very closed-minded statement. It sounds one hundred percent wrong. After all, there are so many other religions with good laws and practices, each with millions of good people who belong to these religions. How can Christianity single itself out from all other religions and say all the others are wrong and they're the only ones who are right? It sounds so wrong."

"Let's try a little experiment," says Leo. Then he turns to George. "George, may I please have a piece of paper and a pencil?" In a jiffy, George is in and out of the house; he places them in front of Leo who draws a line down the center of the page and places it in front of Cameron.

"Every religion has a point of completion...a goal," explains Leo. "Some call it heaven, some call it nirvana, and others say it's being with god, or becoming one with god; some even believe they become gods. Whatever the case, it is the final goal." Leo points to the paper. "On the right side of the paper, I want you to write down every religion you're familiar with and the process...the system...the *Way* they believe they will reach their goal."

Cameron takes the pencil and gets busy. Vanessa, his wife, and some of the other guests help him, making a game of it.

"You need to break it up into two categories; the ones who believe in reincarnation and the ones who don't," says someone.

"There is a difference between the Buddhists in India and the Buddhists in the Far East," someone points out.

"Yeah, but don't they all believe the same?" asks another.

"I don't think so."

"Is Hinduism a religion? I thought it was a cover name for a bunch of religions."

"I always thought Confucianism was more of a philosophy than a religion."

"Should you count Witchcraft; I mean…do people still do that stuff?"

"I tell you, Satanism is a real religion; look it up!"

"I don't know if you can count some of this *New Age* stuff that's been popping up in the past few years. After all, it's just a rehash of some of the old stuff; isn't it?"

On and on they go till Cameron hands the page back to Leo – the entire right side is full.

"Let's see," says Leo, running his finger up and down the right side of the page. "It looks as if you covered a good amount of ground. Why don't we make separate list of all the *Ways* these religions suggest we get to reach our goal."

The list consists of: Being a good person – Leading a good life – Treating others well – these seem the main three. Then there is: Giving to the poor – Going to a church or temple – Praying – Meditating – Sacrificing – Suffering – Fasting – Pilgrimages – Reincarnating – Studying Holy writings – Following Holy beings (living and dead, seen and unseen) – Good deeds and works.

"That's some list we have here," says Leo. He hands the page back to Cameron. "Now, on the left side of the page I want you to list all the religions that want you to do nothing for your salvation."

"Nothing…?" Cameron asks, sounding confused.

"Yes, nothing," Leo confirms. He points to the list on the right. "What religions say all the *Ways* you've listed here are useless when it comes to salvation and there's nothing you can do to earn your salvation?"

"Useless…nothing?" Cameron echoes.

"Yes, nothing you can do; all your efforts will come up short!"

"That sounds hopeless and frightening," says Cameron.

"It's not hopeless," says Leo, "because the next question says it all. What religion says all you need do for salvation someone else already did, and all you need do is believe and trust in Him?"

Leo takes the pencil and writes on the left side of the page.

"There's only one religion that makes this claim, and that religion is Christianity! Jesus Christ paid the price for our salvation…a price we could never pay. All we need do is confess our shortcomings, turn from them, and accept the gift he offers.

"Compared with other religions Christianity stands alone. That's why Christians claim it as the only *Way*. What you called one-hundred percent wrong is now at a fifty-fifty percentage. It's either true or it's false; it's either right or it's wrong."

"Which is it?" asks Cameron. "Is it the truth?"

"That is what only you can find out," replies Leo.

From that point on the conversation does not only heat-up, it sizzles. Questions about Christianity fill the air.

"I don't get this *Trinity* bit. How is it you can have one God, but then he's three different guys?"

"If God is love and all-powerful then why does he allow bad things to happen? Why doesn't he stop them? Just look at the world…it's a mess!"

"Do good people go to hell? I don't get it! Is Gandhi in hell?"

"It wouldn't surprise me if 666 is a computer chip. They've got them so small now they can put them under your skin."

"Of course, I want to go to heaven, just like everyone else does; but if my cats are not there, I'm not going. It wouldn't be heaven without them."

George looks over at Jesus sitting next to him; His hands folded in front of Him; He is smiling.

"I love this, George, I really do."

****

In the midst of all the deep searching conversation, again someone makes the observation, "The children…I don't hear the children!" One of the women points to Patricia. The children are at her feet, listening to her every word.

"She certainly has a way with children."

"She does beyond a doubt," Jesus declares. "In fact, I know she is thinking about starting a baby-sitting service."

"Really…I need to get her phone number," a woman takes a pen and pad from her purse, starting toward Patricia. "I could use a reliable sitter, too," says another. "Wait for me," says yet another.

"One of the men said you're a good baby-sitter."

It takes Patricia aback. "Well, I was thinking about doing it again."

"And you live right here in the neighborhood; how good is that?" one of the woman sighs. "Do you have any plans for next Friday night?"

"I've only been thinking about it," repeats Patricia.

A small child sitting at her feet jumps up, wrapping her arms around Patricia's legs. "Oh, say yes, Auntie Patricia! It would be so awesome if you were my sitter!"

"That settles that," says the child's mother.

"What about Saturday?" one of the other mothers asks. "Are you open next Saturday?"

The sun begins to set, sunset colors fill the sky. The heated discussion around the main table is calming down. Many seem impressed with Leo's ability to put many Christian ideas and beliefs across clearly. He does not leave a wake of new believers, still he leaves them wanting for more; and that's half the battle won.

One by one, each household takes their casserole dish; make their apologies, say their good-byes, and start to leave. George, Martha and Jesus stand at the gate thanking every guest for coming.

"You know, this discussion is not over yet, not by a long shot," Cameron says, smiling and shaking George's hand.

"Whenever you're ready," George says. "If you and your wife ever get a mind to, it would be our pleasure for you both to be our guest one Sunday at our church."

"Think of it this way," Martha adds, "You've traveled the world, swam the Gangues, climbed the Himalayas to find truth, and never took the time to check out the local church. Maybe, what you've been looking for has been under your nose all this time."

"We may just do that," says Cameron.

The two women hug and the men shake hands, once more.

"Thank you for a wonderful day," says Vanessa as she and Cameron walk off.

"I need to know the recipe for that divine fish we had!" Old Mrs. Cradle asks, taking hold of Martha's hands.

"I had nothing to do with it, Mrs. Cradle. You need to ask our houseguest, Jesus."

"It's very simple," Jesus says. "Make sure you get your coals white-hot, and dampen your grill with oil so the fish doesn't stick. Then, in a large bowl, mix olive oil, lemon juice, salt, pepper, and fresh oregano. While the fish is cooking, dip an olive branch into the mixture and continually brush the fish."

"An olive branch...! Where am I supposed to get an olive branch?"

"Our friend is a bit old school, Mrs. Cradle. Just use anything you normally baste meats with."

"Do I know you?" Mrs. Cradle says, eyeing Jesus carefully. "You look awfully familiar."

"We met years ago, just for a moment," Jesus says. "It was the year you graduated from Chrisom College."

Mrs. Cradle bursts into laughter. "Young man do you know when that was? Do you know how old I am? You're not even half my age! There's no way we could have met that year."

"Yes, we did," Jesus replies. "Your dear, sweet, sainted husband mentioned me to you time and time again over the years of your marriage, even up to the day he died. Now, I want you to go home and take the box of his letters out from under the bed and read them again. See how many times he mentions me…Jesus. But most of all, pay attention to what he says about me."

Mrs. Cradle walks quietly away, spellbound; her head turns, looking back into the eyes of Jesus. She looks at him constantly till she turns the corner.

Next to leave are Leo and Dianne.

"Thanks for inviting us, that was such a lovely party," says Dianne.

"Thank you for coming," George says. "It wouldn't have been the same without you. Especially, without your husband; he was the man of the hour, a real hero."

"Yes, he was, wasn't he," says Dianne with pride. It had been years since she spoke of her husband with pride; it feels good.

"That was quite a stand you made this afternoon," George says.

"All head-knowledge, nothing more," replies Leo.

"And certainly a good amount of heart-knowledge," George responds.

"Not one word came from my heart!" Leo insists.

"I don't understand," George says. "When a saved person…"

"What makes you think I'm saved?" Leo interrupts.

"But I thought…"

"Well, you thought wrong," continues Leo. "I told you when we first met; if there even is such a thing as salvation, it's not for me."

"Salvation is for everyone," Martha insists.

"Thank you for your hospitality," Leo says as he walks away.

The beaming pride and smile on Dianne's face slowly disappears. "I'm sorry; I told you he's not what you call the social type."

Leo storms off with Dianne following close behind.

Next is Patricia; the small woman walks slowly forward, smiling shyly at Jesus.

"I already know the answer," says Patricia. "But I think I best say it; and I know you deserve to hear it. I'm sorry, will you please forgive me?"

"I'm glad to hear you say it," Jesus remarks, smiling.

"Now, if you'll please excuse me," says Patricia, "I need to go home and clean house…both figuratively as well as literally."

Jesus is silent and still smiling.

With a burst of tears, she falls into his arms; He holds her close.

"I truly am sorry," she says, her face buried in his chest. "I'm sorry for the way I've been and things I've said. I do love you…I do!"

"I know you do, Patricia; and I will always love you."

He takes her face in His hands and kisses her forehead.

"Now stop your crying. We've known each other for so long and too well for there to be tears. Remember, I am with you…always."

Through her tears and a smile, Patricia makes her way back to her little garage apartment.
Jesus turns to see George and Martha nearly in tears themselves.
"Is there any fish left?" He asks.

Nineteen

Saturday Night

Mimi

Mimi has always had a slight weight problem. Nothing serious, as a child they called it baby fat. When she was a teenager, they called her big boned. She was always popular especially with the boys, always going out on dates. Yet the world demands perfection even it cannot deliver. Now as a mature woman most would consider her voluptuous, and she was happy with that, but not her doctor. She'd tried everything. She'd been on an all-grapefruit diet, an all hard-boiled egg diet, low carb, low fat, and at times starvation, which her doctor advised against. Recently, she was into juice, only healthy, fresh made juices.

Mimi places six carrots, two celery sticks, and one red delicious apple into her juicer, turning it on. The thick orange liquid fills the glass. She places the glass on the kitchen table, and returns to the sink to clean the juicer. She can never concentrate clearly on a matter while surrounded by clutter.

She sits down, takes a sip of her concoction, and opens her new Bible to page one.

"In the beginning..." she whispers. She reads on, understanding some of it very clearly; though most of it puffs like a vapor through her mind – making little sense.

She decides to skip ahead a few chapters; but that's even worse. All those countries, armies, battles, tossing lamb's blood around, and cutting up cows and throwing the fat on sacrificial fires – it all makes no sense to Mimi.

"Someone's going to have to explain this all to me," she whines. "They call this the 'Good Book'? It reads like *War and Peace*; with a heck of a lot more war than there is peace!"

She examines the few pictures in the book. "Beards...all the men have beards. Not well groomed either. Beards down their chests. I couldn't love a man who looked like that. Kissing him would be like sticking your face in a bird's nest. Yuck!"

Turning the pages, she reads ahead a little farther, and realizes it is in two parts. "The Old Testament and the New Testament...what's a testament? I guess it's like what they do in courtrooms, but I doubt that."

The New Testament reads much more easily for her. It is still slow going at first but it begins moving faster and reads smoother.

"So here's where they keep the peace parts," she says, sounding pleased.

She realizes she hasn't taken a sip from her drink. Not wanting it to loose its potency, she drinks it down in a few gulps.

The New Testament isn't all peaceful, but a whole lot better than the old. When she gets to the words written in red her jaw drops.

"These must be the words Jesus spoke," she thinks out loud.

She reads everything in red; some parts even twice, and she understands every word, sentence, and parable. The red words sink into her brain and take root; she feels it growing in her heart.

Her finger moves over the words faster and faster, as she grows more excited.

"I didn't know that! I didn't know that!" she keeps repeating. "Why didn't someone tell me all this before?" she announces, sounding slightly perturbed. "If I'm just finding this out; how many other people don't know this? Someone has to tell them! I have to tell them!"

Twenty

Prime Time

"So, what is it you like to do on a Saturday night?" Jesus asks.

George and Martha look at each other for an answer, George responds, "We usually watch some television."

"Yes," Martha says. "I don't want to miss my show."

"Your show…?" Jesus asks. "You have your own show on television?"

"No," Martha laughs. "I only mean I don't want to miss my favorite show."

"And what is that?"

"It's about a group of shipwrecked people on a deserted island. You'll like it."

Martha turns the television on; they all take a seat.

To both George and Martha's astonishment, Jesus watches the show with great interest, although the commercials through him off.

"I don't understand; is this part of the story? One moment they're collecting firewood, the next this woman is washing her hair."

"It's a commercial," George says. "It's what the networks broadcast between the show's acts to produce income. People pay money to hawk their goods."

"But there was no warning; it just appears on the screen."

"I know," George laughs.

"I must say, she looks extraordinarily happy just by washing her hair," Jesus declares. "And what's this?"

"A car commercial," Martha says.

"They look happy, too. And this…?"

"…breakfast cereal."

"More happiness…"

Commercial after commercial appears on the screen with more happy faces.

"How many commercials do they show? I've nearly forgotten what we were watching."

The show starts again; the marooned people collect firewood; no more happy faces.

Jesus watches intently and silently to the rest of the show.

At the end of the show, the names of the actors and those who took part in the production fly from bottom to top across the screen, to fast for any average person to read.

"So, what did you think?" George asks, turning off the television.

Jesus remains absorbed in thought. "It was interesting, clearly well written, acted, and produced. I thought it strange every commercial portrayed a way to happiness. I ask you…where is the Father?"

"The Father…?" George asks.

"Yes, where is God in all this. The commercials claim happiness through things. Everyone knows that's false, yet they continue in that direction. It's a lie; there is no happiness outside of a relationship with the Father."

George and Martha listen, and for once realize even a simple television show they shouldn't view lightly. There are more important things in life.

"So, what comes next on a Saturday night?" Jesus asks.

"We like to walk down to the Sweet Shop and get some ice-cream," George states.

"Ice-cream…!" Jesus echoes. "I've never had any; I've always wanted to try some."

"Then, what are we waiting for?" George says.

George is just turning the key to lock the front door of the house when a car pulls to the front. It's Mimi; she comes rushing up the walkway with her Bible in her hand.

"Where's that young man who gave me this Bible?" demands Mimi.

"That would be me," Jesus says.

"You're not him," Mimi says. "I mean, you look something like him; only you look different."

"Have you been reading your Bible?" He asks.

"Yes, I have!"

"Well, that would explain it."

Martha comes walking over. "Mimi, what's the matter?"

"This book," Mimi says. "I've been reading it all-day long; mostly the stuff in red. Why didn't anyone tell me this stuff? All my life I've never heard any of this! I'm…" Mimi stops for a moment and then continues. "I was just about to tell you how old I am. Let's just say I'm a grown women and I've never heard any of this!"

Martha hangs her head down for a moment in shame, and then she looks at her friend squarely.

"Mimi, I'm sorry. I should have said something, sooner. I just didn't want to lose you. I was so afraid."

"Afraid of what?" asks Mimi.

"I don't know…I just was afraid."

"Don't you be," says Mimi, reaching out and hugging Martha. "This is the best day of my life! Only, I'm confused."

"Confused…?" Martha asks.

"This book is incredible! For every answer I learn, I've got two more questions. I don't know what to think."

"Maybe, we should have a Bible study class?" says Martha, excited she said it.

"That sounds great!" exclaims Mimi.

Then, Martha feels the hand of Jesus touch her shoulder; and in an instant she knows what she needs to say.

"Mimi…would you like to give your life to Christ?"

Mimi looks at her for a moment, blankly; then she smiles.

"Yes…no…I mean. Oh, I don't know what I mean. It's so confusing."

Martha takes hold of her hands.

"Why don't we go back in the house and talk about it." Martha turns to George and Jesus. "If you two gentlemen will please excuse us…?"

They watch the two women walk arm in arm back into the house.

"Well, George, it looks as if it's just the two of us."

The two men walk off.

Less than a block away, a dark figure approaches them; passing under a streetlamp, the light shows it to be Leo.

"Are all your days this busy?" George asks Jesus.

Jesus just smiles.

Leo walks up to them; ignoring Jesus, he stands in front of George.

"We need to talk," says Leo.

"I'd love to," George says, pointing to Jesus, "but I promised our houseguest we'd…"

Before he can say another word, Jesus reaches out, tugging at George's sleeve.

"It's all right, George. I can go to the sweetshop alone."

"No, I can't let you do that," George says.

"Oh, I'll be fine." Jesus looks at Leo. "Besides, I think this is more important than ice-cream."

George takes his wallet, pulls out a five-dollar bill, handing it to Jesus.

"Here, take this; you'll need it to pay for the ice-cream. The shop is three blocks straight ahead. Now, you're sure you don't want me to go with you?"

"Relax, George. I'm a grown boy; I can take care of myself."

Twenty-one

Mimi and Martha

Sitting at the breakfast table in the kitchen, Martha put on a pot of coffee. Mimi thumbs through her Bible. Martha prays a silent prayer as she pours coffee. She prays the Holy Spirit will intervene.

"So, Mimi, tell me what has you confused."

Mimi holds her coffee cup in front of her lips, takes a sip, looking over the rim at Martha.

"Like I said, it's all so new to me. It goes against everything I knew about life; yet somehow it rings true for me."

"What's changed?" Martha asks.

"Well, for one thing, I've always believed there is a God, but I never really thought much about it. I always thought everything would work out on its own. All you have to do is be a good person and lead a good life, right? Wrong!

"Now, I'm not only sure there is a God, but I even know his name and what He's like and what He expects of me and what I can expect of Him. It's all so strange. Everything doesn't work out on its own, like I thought or how we might want it to; I need to be involved with my life and salvation, and I need to form a connection with this God...somehow!"

"Do you understand how you form this connection?" Martha asks.

"That's just it," says Mimi. "I've always believed in something like a heaven and a hell. I mean, I always thought good people get rewarded and bad people find punishment. However, that's not exactly as it is; there's more to it than that. Sure, we need to do our best to be good; but how good can we be; after all we're just human beings, and you know what stinkers they can be."

Martha just smiles as she listens to her friend's testimony unfold.

"I always believed if you're a good person and help others then you go to heaven. I know I'm not perfect; but I thought if I did more good than bad it would all balance out somehow and I'd be welcomed in heaven.

"Only that's like knocking on the door of a large mansion belonging to a rich person. He answers the door and says 'Hello, may I help you?' and you say, 'Yeah, I've come here to live in this lovely mansion with you'.

"Now, you know he's going to say something like, 'Why should I let you live here with me?' and you say 'Because I'm such a good person.' You just know that's not going to cut it. 'I'm glad you're a good person', he says, 'but only family members live here with me'. So you ask him, 'Well, how does one become a family member?' 'That's easy', he says, 'all you have to do is be perfect. After all, this mansion is perfect and I'm perfect; so it only makes sense my entire family who live here with me be perfect'.

"What can you say to that? Tell him you're a good person who will keep trying to be better and better till finally you too become perfect. Forget it; it will never happen! So what's a person to do?"

Martha is still smiling. "I don't know, Mimi, you tell me."

"Well, you need to understand what it means to be perfect. Perfect is to be sinless; and honey, that sure isn't me or anyone else I know. But Jesus was sinless; and when He took the sins of the world on Him and offered Himself as a sacrifice, all those sins He paid for. All a person needs to do is accept Him and the sacrifice He made and you've got a clean slate. Then the man upstairs will see you as perfect, at least in his eyes, and worthy of living in his mansion as a family member...a child of God. I guess if you had to sum it up in one word it would be *Adoption*. That's it! Through Christ, you are made perfect and the Father will take you in as His child to live with Him in heaven, forever. Am I making any sense?"

Martha's smile grows larger. "Mimi, I thought you said you felt confused?"

Mimi goes silent for a moment, tilting her head slightly. "You know, I'm not a bit confused." A look of surprise and shear joy comes over Mimi. "Martha," she shouts, "I'm not confused!" Tears begin to form in her eyes.

"Then you want to accept Jesus as your savior?" Martha asks.

"Most positively...right here, right now...forever and ever!"

"Just tell Him in your own words, from your heart," Martha says.

"No," says Mimi, "I want to do this kneeling; will you kneel with me, Martha."

"Of course; I'd be proud to."

The two women fall to their knees on the kitchen floor, folding their hands in prayer. There are tears streaming down their cheeks.

"Hello, Lord, it's me, Mimi. I know I'm a sinner, so imperfect and unworthy. I repent of my sins and I accept this gift you offer, the gift of your one and only begotten son. The blood He shed for me, I accept you, Jesus, as my Lord and Savior. I thank you and praise you forever and ever!"

Mimi opens her eyes, reaching out for Martha.

"Was that all right?" she asks.

Martha can barely see Mimi through her tears.

"That was just fine, Mimi, just fine."

Again, Martha says a silent prayer; this time it's a prayer of thanksgiving. Earlier, she prayed for the right words; yet Mimi found salvation with nary a word spoken from her. God never stops to amaze her. Still, she feels blessed to be there, an essential part of what happened. She thanks God for allowing her to be part of it.

"There's still so much I want and need to understand," says Mimi.

"That will come in time," Martha reassures her. "You see, the world says 'I'll believe it when I see it' but Christianity says, "First, believe it, and then you will see it."

Later, standing in the doorway, the two women say goodnight.

"Thank you so much, Martha; I don't think I could have done it without you."

"Of course you could; but I'm proud to be here for you."

"Do me a favor," says Mimi.

"Anything..." Martha replies.

"Do me a favor and tell that young man who gave me this Bible...tell him thank you."

"I'm sure he knows, but I'll tell Him so, personally."

"Thank you, my dear friend." Mimi throws her arms around Martha.

Martha whispers in her ear, "Welcome to the family."

"My dear sweet sister," Mimi whispers back.

Standing in the doorway, Mimi strikes a pose, her hand on her hip, and in true Mae-West-Fashion says her good-bye.

"Well...see ya in church."

The two women fall once more into each others arms, breaking into laughter and tears.

Twenty-two

Leo and George

George and Leo walk back toward George's house. Then he remembers, "Oh, wait, my wife has a visitor. I know...we can go into the garage and talk...I use it for a workshop."

However, Leo is in too much of a hurry to wait. He stops under the light of a streetlamp. George stops, turning to Leo with a questioning look.

"George, sorry to do this; I just need to get something off my chest. All that religion talk today got me thinking."

"I don't understand, Leo," George says. "Having all those answers and defending the Christian Faith; then saying you're not saved and salvation isn't for you. I just don't understand, Leo."

Leo stops for a moment, looking deeply concerned, doing his best to put his thoughts in order.

"It all has to do with forgiveness, George."

"Forgiveness...?"

"Yeah, forgiveness...some things are just too bad...too evil...too sinful to forgive."

"Nonsense, Leo, no sin is that great!"

"Oh, that's where you're wrong, George! There are things in this world most people never hear of or, thank God, even think of; still they exist."

George is silent. He realizes this is not a debate by Leo; it's a confession.

Leo continues, "If the light of God is so great, it only goes to say there is an equally great darkness...a darkness void of all light...void of God. There are acts people perform in darkness that have no name; inhuman acts that haunt a man's memory till his only hope is to go insane. There is no forgiveness for these acts."

"You're wrong, Leo; there's no darkness dark enough to defuse the light of God, Darkness isn't real, it's just the absence of light. When you turn on the light, the darkness is no more. In the same way, spiritual darkness is just the absence of God, but the light of Our Lord shatters any darkness no matter how dark! If we accept Jesus Christ as our savior, there is no sin so terrible God will not forgive it!"

"God...? Who said anything about the forgiveness of God?" says Leo.

George does a double-take.

"It's not the forgiveness of God I doubt; it's my forgiveness that can never happen. I'm my own stumbling block! I'm the one who can never bring himself to forgive the sins I've committed!"

George stands still, staring at Leo in disbelief. He says a quick unspoken prayer for guidance.

"I'm sure you feel that way, Leo; thinking about your past and all the sins you've committed. Only none of them compare with the sin you're committing this very moment!"

Now it's Leo's turn to do a double-take. A cold questioning stare comes over Leo's face. "What are you talking about?"

"I'm talking about pride, Leo. The first original sin…pride! It was pride that caused the fall of the Angel Lucifer when he wanted to be as God. It was pride that caused the fall of man when Adam and Eve believed Satan's lies that they too could be like God. But not you; you don't want to be like God, you think you're better than God! God will forgive you; but your standards are higher. You'll never forgive yourself! But it's not your forgiveness that counts…it's God's. By not accepting his forgiveness, you're saying his offering of his son's life was nothing more than a waste…a wasted life…a waste of blood. By not accepting forgiveness, you're saying you're better than God! Pride, that's what it is. You're not God, Leo; you never will be. None of us can even come close!"

They both stand silent for a moment. Leo looks upward. The light from the streetlamp shines on his face. George sees the pain in Leo's eyes.

"Oh, my God…what have I done? Oh, my God…please forgive me. I had no right to say such things. I'm sorry; please forgive me!"

Leo takes hold of both of George's arms, gripping tightly.

"No, you're right; I have been so full of pride. I've been so wrong and blind for far too long." Tears begin to stream down his face. "If only God could forgive me, now!"

"Of course, He will…if you will."

Deep inside Leo he knew the answer, nevertheless, for some reason due to human weakness he just has to ask, "It isn't too late?"

"It's never too late, as long as there's life. It's all there for you, just waiting for you. Think of it this way, you're well versed, what does the Gospel of John 3:16 say?"

Leo thinks for a moment. "For God so loved the world…"

"Stop right there and say it again. For the world, Leo, it doesn't say for just him or her, or them, or us. It says the world, that means everyone, and that includes you, too. Now say it again, only this time substitute your name for the world."

Leo starts again, "For God so loved Leo that He gave his one and only begotten Son…"
George urges him on, "Go on, Leo."

"That if me, Leo, believeth in Him, I will not perish, but have eternal life."

"That's the truth; it's true for all believers."

Leo loosens his grip. He spreads his arms out and again looks upward, only this time he looks passed the streetlamp to the sky, passed the moon and stars. He looks to heaven.

"Oh, Father, I'm sorry. Forgive my sinfulness and my foolishness. I turn my back on my sins. Take my heart of stone and make it flesh. With all my heart, mind, and soul, I accept your son Jesus Christ as my personal savior and I dedicate my life to you!"

After a long moment of silence, George speaks, "So, how do you feel, now?"

Leo takes a moment to take stock of himself, smiling at George. "I feel…I feel…free!"

"You are free, Leo."

Strong emotions sweep over Leo like a mighty ocean wave, washing him clean. He falls into George's arms. "Thank you, George, thank you."

"It's my pleasure."

"Oh, I just thought of something," Leo says, backing off. "I need to tell Dianne. When she hears this she'll be so happy!"

"Then what are you doing here?" George laughs. "Go tell her, right now! Run to her, Leo, run to her!"

"Thanks again, George," says Leo as he runs off into the dark.

George stands in the light of the streetlamp. It feels warm. He watches as Leo disappears into the dark. Then he looks up again, passed the streetlamp to the sky, passed the moon and stars. He looks to heaven.

"Thank you, Lord."

He hears Leo's voice shouting at him from down the block, from the darkness, "See you in church!"

Twenty-three

Pop's Sweet Shop

Harvey

Ice-cream was life to Harvey Montello; top of the food groups. As a child he traded all his Halloween candy with his friends for pennies, nickels and dimes – at a loss – just so he could buy an ice-cream cone. His mother never baked a Birthday Cake for him; they always sent out for an ice-cream cake. He anticipated the removal of his tonsils as if it were a holiday, knowing he could have his fill of ice-cream.

He showed no preference of flavors. Vanilla: creamy and smooth, Chocolate: rich and dreamy, Strawberry: exotic and fruity, and a Banana Split: Heaven.

In his teens, Harvey's love of ice-cream became obvious to all by the pounds he now bore. Still, he wore them well; and they helped him get on the football team – defense. It was the same in college; a stocky guy such as he was needed on the line.

When the war broke out, Harvey enlisted. Unlike many of the other soldiers, Harvey didn't smoke, didn't gamble, didn't drink, nor did he chase women. The largest portion of his pay he sent home to his mother; the rest he spent at the commissary on ice-cream.

When they shipped him overseas, Harvey lost quite a bit of weight. The life of a soldier is a physical one. They design food rations to be lightweight to carry, nutritious enough to sustain good health with a flavor that made you yearn for anything other than what you were eating. Of course, on the battlefield there is no ice-cream!

At night, when he and his comrades sat in their trenches up to their ankles in mud, drenched by freezing rain, they spoke of their dreams.

"When I get home, I'm getting me some of that Kansas City Beef and grill it till it's well done. I'm going to eat it with a baked potato...nothing else," says Duffy from New Jersey.

"I got a job waiting for me on my Daddy's ranch. I'm going to work my butt off all week long; but on Friday I'm going into town. I'm going to raise hell; and ain't anybody going to see me till Monday!" said Tex.

"Not me," said Holliman. "I've been saving all my dough. First thing I'm going to do is put it down on an engagement ring and I'm going to drop to my knees and propose to Mary Sue. Then I'm going back to college and..."

"What if Mary Sue says no?" laughs Duffy.

Holliman reaches into his backpack, pulling out a handful of letters. "That girl's been writing me nearly everyday; that girl is primed!" They all burst into laughter. Holliman continues, "Then I'm going back to college, get me a good trade, and then find me a nice job, somewhere. Then I'm buying us a nice little house. Me and Mary Sue are going to settle in like two badgers in a badger hole; and have us a mess of kids, and grandkids, too…great grandkids…God willing."

"What are you going to do when you get home?" Tex asks Harvey. Harvey just smiles; this was a question he need not think long for an answer – he knew the answer all his life.

"Boys, when I get back I'm going to march up and down Main Street till I find me an empty store…one on a corner…and I'm going to open me up an ice-cream shop. It's going to be the sweetest little sweet shop you ever saw. It's all going to be homemade. I'm going to make all the ice-cream myself. I'm going to have more flavors than you can shake a stick at. I might even make an *avocado* flavor…who knows."

"You can't make ice-cream from avocados," says Duffy.

"How do you know till you try?" Harvey insists.

"Well, it can't be any worse than the crud they feed us here," says Tex, they all laugh.

Late at night, each in his sleeping bag, trying their best to sleep, Harvey would pray. His mother who he considered the most Holy woman alive taught him how to pray.

"To remain pure, you pray to the Blessed Virgin. When you want to make something with your hands, you pray to Saint Joseph…he was a carpenter. When you travel, you pray to Saint Christopher. When things seem hopeless, you pray to Saint Jude."

Harvey wondered if there was a patron saint for ice-cream.

After the war, Harvey stayed true to his dream. He promenaded down Main Street till he found just the right vacant corner store; and he opened the sweetest little sweet shop you ever laid eyes on. He called it *Pop's Sweet Shop*. Now, the name Pop would lead a person to believe the shop was owned and run by a much older man. Harvey was still young, but he planned to grow into the name, in time.

****

It's a slow night at Pop's. Harvey sits in the backroom going over his books. The years have been kind to him. The sweet shop is a great success, a landmark in the town. Years earlier, Harvey married Helen, a great lover of ice-cream, as well. They live in a fine house, raised two sons, now married and settled down; raising his grandchildren that Harvey envisioned so many years ago. He feels proud of his accomplishments. The sweet shop made it all possible. Life is good. It is as sweet as ice-cream.

After so many years, Harvey is now truly Pop of Pop's Sweet Shop. He looks the part. He's a chubby, balding, ever smiling, little man who looks good in a white apron.

The tiny bell over the door chimes. Harvey comes out to the front, smiling, to greet his costumer.

Jesus walks to the counter and hoists himself up onto one of the stools. Harvey stands behind the counter, wiping his hands across the front of his apron, smiling.

"The name's Harvey, but most people call me 'Pop'. What can I do you for?"

"Well, Pop, I'd like to have some ice-cream."

"Then you've come to the right place," Pop says. "We've got the best in town. What will it be a bowl or cone?"

"Cone...?" Jesus questions.

"Yeah, cone...we got regular, sugar, or waffle."

"I think it best I just stick to something safe...I'll have a bowl."

"What flavor would you like? We got vanilla, French vanilla, chocolate, chocolate chip, rum raisin, rocky road, coffee mocha, strawberry, cherry bomb, and this week's special...cookie dough."

Jesus leans forward and whispers, "To tell you the truth, Pop, I don't know what to order; I've never eaten ice-cream before."

Pops takes a moment to react. He gives a double-take and sways back and forth as if he's about to faint. "Nah...you're kidding me! A man your age and you ain't ever had ice-cream?"

"No never...honestly."

"Really...?"

"Really..."

Pop takes another moment to think. "Well, if that's the case, I'd say start off with the basics either a scoop of vanilla or chocolate."

"I don't know," Jesus says. "Which is better?"

"Hard to say," Pop says. "Tell you what, since this is your first time, why don't you buy a scoop of vanilla and I'll throw in a scoop of chocolate on the house."

"Sounds like a deal," Jesus says, smiling.

Pop takes a bowl, an ice-cream scoop, and gets to work. All the while mumbling, "Unbelievable...ain't ever had ice-cream...unbelievable!"

Jesus looks around; he is the only customer at this late hour. He eyes the wall behind Pop. There is an American Flag, photos of a young Harvey on the opening day of the Sweet Shop, and a picture frame containing the first dollar bill the shop earned.

On the lowest, farthest place on the wall is a small crucifix with dry brown pieces of palm wrapped around it.

"So, Pop..." Jesus says, pointing to the crucifix. "So, you're a Christian?"

"Sure am, born and raised."

Next to the crucifix are a dozen painted portraits on small cards.

"Who are all those people?" Jesus asks.

"Those are saints...my favorite ones. There's Saint Anthony and Saint Jude...and that one's Saint Francis of Assisi...he's my favorite of my favorites. They're all great and holy saints. Except that one, of course; that there's the Virgin Mary...the Mother of God."

"If God always existed, how can He have a mother?" Jesus asks.

"You got a point there," Pop says, laughing. "Well, anyway, she was the mother of Jesus. She's more powerful than any of the others combined. You pray to her and she'll get it done."

"So you pray to Mary and the Saints?" Jesus asks. "Why…?"

"They intervene for you. They're the go-betweens for you and God."

"Then why not just go and speak straight to God?" Jesus asks.

"Oh, you can't do that! That's why we have Mary and the Saints! That way you have someone to plead you're case. You pray to them and they talk to God for you. Let's face it; they're Saints…more holy than you or me. They'll get it done for you."

Just then, the bell over the front door rings; a small girl of eight or nine steps over to the stool two down from Jesus – she jumps up.

"I'd like one scoop of cookie dough on a sugar cone, please."

"What's your name?" Jesus asks, spinning on his stool to face her.

"Melissa."

"Well, Melissa, has anyone ever told you how beautiful you are?"

She just giggles and smiles revealing two missing front teeth.

A moment later, Pop presents the girl with her ice-cream cone. "Here you go, little lady." Then he places a bowl and spoon in front of Jesus. "Here you go, sir…enjoy."

From the first mouthful, Jesus' eyes go wide with delight.

"Delicious…" He says as He alternates between chocolate and vanilla.

"It's good, ain't it?" Pop says, beaming with pride.

Melissa silently works away at her cone.

"I'm interested," Pop says. "Tell me, which one you like better, the vanilla or chocolate?"

Jesus doesn't say a word, he continues to eat.

"I asked which one you like better?"

Jesus puts down his spoon, turns his stool to face the little girl.

"Melissa, tell Pop I think his ice-cream is delicious."

The girl looks up at Pop. "He says he thinks that…"

"Yeah…yeah…I heard." Pop directs his question to Jesus. "But which one do you like best?"

"Melissa, tell Pop, I'm partial to the vanilla; but when I taste the chocolate, somehow I forget what the vanilla tasted like."

"He says…"

"Yeah, I said, I heard! Say listen, buddy, quit talking to the kid and talk to me. I'm the one asking the questions."

"Melissa, please tell Pop that I…"

Pop grabs the bowl of ice-cream, pulling it away from Jesus.

"Say, buddy, what are you trying to pull? I talk to you and you talk to the kid! Don't you think that's disrespectful?"

Jesus looks him squarely in the eye. "Yes, I do. I think it's very disrespectful!"

"Then why are you doing it?" asks Pop.

A gentle, loving look comes over the face of Jesus – He speaks.

"On the first Good Friday, the sky went dark and the rain fell. People dropped to their knees as the earth trembled. With a crack of thunder, the curtain in the temple separating God from his people for hundreds of years tore from ceiling to floor. The veil was lifted."

Jesus points to the portraits.

"These people were all good and Godly people, but they're dead. The dead can neither hear nor help the living. What was the sacrifice for, if not to make a direct path to God? Harvey, what loving father doesn't want to hear the words of his children from their own lips? What loving father doesn't listen to his children's requests and not want to fill them. He is beyond doubt a loving Father to all who call on Him as their Father."

Jesus stands and lays the five dollar bill on the counter.

"No…no…it's on me." Pop says, pushing the bill back to Jesus.

"Thank you for the ice-cream."

"No, thank you," Pop insists.

Standing at the Sweet Shop entrance, Jesus turns around for one last look before he leaves. Pop is taking down the small portrait cards from the wall. Melissa smiles her toothless smile. Jesus smiles back. He turns and is gone.

Twenty-four

Back Home

George is halfway to the Sweet Shop when he meets Jesus coming in the opposite direction.

"Oh, hi, I was just coming to get you," George says.

"No need, thank you, though. Oh, here's your money back; thank you, again."

"Didn't you have your ice-cream?"

"Yes, but the owner refused to let me pay."

"Why, did he recognize you?" George asks.

"No, however he finally recognized himself."

George felt tempted to ask for a clarification of what He meant; except George knew any explanation was sure to go far over his head.

"So, how did you like eating ice-cream?"

"It was all I expected and more," Jesus says. "So, how did it go with Leo?"

"It was all I expected and more," George echoes.

"You need to follow up with him," Jesus adds. "He has much head-knowledge only he's still living on milk. Stick close to him until he's weaned and on solid food."

Back at the house, Martha greets them at the front door.

"So, how did it go with Mimi?' Jesus asks her.

"It was wonderful! She accepted Jesus...I mean...she accepted you into her life as her savior."

"That's great!" George says. "Make sure you follow up with her. Stick close to her until she's weaned and ready for solid food."

Jesus looks at George with a side-glance and a slight giggle. "You took the words right out of my mouth, George."

"So, what do you want to do next?" Martha asks, looking to Jesus, sounding slightly hyperactive from all the excitement.

"I don't know about you two, but I'm ready to call it a day; I'm tired," Jesus announces. "I'll just go to my room, if you don't mind. Tomorrow's church, isn't it? I'll see you both in the morning."

"What time do you want us to wake you?" George asks.

"Don't worry, I'll be up," Jesus replies.

In their bedroom, Martha and George do their usual nightly ritual. They get into their pajamas, brush their teeth. George tips his head back, putting a few drops into his eyes to ward off dry-eye, which he always gets from a night's sleep. Martha's regiment is a bit more intense. She brushes out her hair, counting two hundred strokes and then ties it back from her face with ribbon. Then she moisturizes her skin, mostly her face with gels and creams and other mystical potions.

Back in the bedroom, they stand on their side of the bed, respectively, and pull back the covers. At first, it seems like any other night; but it's not, this night is different. Without a single spoken word, as if on queue, they look to each other, knowing what to do. For the first time during their marriage, George and Martha kneel at the edge of their bed, giving thanks to God.

In bed, they reach out and turn off the lamps on their nightstands. They turn over and hold each other close. They are so tired; they barely remember kissing each other goodnight.

"I love you," George whispers.

"I love you, too," Martha responds softly.

Unlike the night before, they fall asleep quickly and deeply.

Twenty-five

Early Sunday Morning

George opens his eyes, staring through the darkness at the ceiling over their bed. For some unexplainable reason, he feels wide-awake.

He glances at the alarm clock; it's a few minutes before sunrise. He closes his eyes hoping to catch a few more minutes of sleep; it's useless. Thoughts of the last two days race through his mind.

He turns to his wife; he can barely make out her sleeping shape lying next to him. He remembers her words and actions over the past few days, and he feels proud...proud to know her, proud to be her life's partner.

"One flesh..." he whispers softly to himself.

He always loved her and their marriage; only now there was something else – he felt honored as well.

He turns the other way and notices a bright light coming through the slit between the window curtains. He knows it's too soon for the sun and wonders what it could be. He gets up to investigate. He pulls the curtains back; he's blinded for a moment by a fierce white light.

When his eyes adjust, he realizes it's the light from the moon. There's a full moon hanging low in the sky. A harvest moon looking unnaturally large, its craters clear to the naked eye; so close George feels he's able to reach out and touch it.

Looking in the eastern direction, there's an orange-yellow light on the horizon – the sun will rise soon.

George looks down at the garden. The moonlight gives the illusion everything's covered in shimmering silver.

George sees Jesus kneeling in the center of the garden. His arms stretched out wide, his head lifted, his eyes closed, his lips are moving. He is praying – the Son is honoring the Father.

The sight moves George so deeply; tears form in his eyes as he falls to his knees. No words can describe his feelings. He feels privileged. He is in awe of the beauty of the moment – more beautiful than anything he ever witnessed in his entire life.

Suddenly, Jesus falls facedown, still praying, humbling Himself all the more.

George's whole body begins to tremble. He turns away; his eyes can no longer withstand the magnificence.

Shaking, he works back up to his feet; he closes the curtains tightly – darkness is all around. He slowly, cautiously makes his way to the bed. He unhurriedly slips under the covers, careful not to wake his wife.

Martha sighs and reaches out to him, speaking in a dozy haze.

"Are you all right?" she asks, her eyes still closed.

"I'm fine," he whispers. "Go back to sleep; everything's just fine."

Feeling reassured, she sighs once more, falling back into a deep slumber.

Still wide awake, George thinks, "Everything is just fine! No it isn't! Nothing is just fine! Nothing will ever be just fine, again! Everything is wonderful... marvelous... awesome... and Holy. That's it...everything is Holy! The entire universe...all creation... i s Holy and filled with love!"

His heart pounds in his chest. Unable to contain himself, George rushes to the window, pulling the curtains open. The silver light of the moon is gone, replaced by the golden sunshine of a new day. Everything is bright, clear and fresh.

He looks to the center of the garden; Jesus is no longer there. George's heart sinks, he feels as if it were breaking. Then he sees something that makes his spirit soar.

There in the center of the garden is a fully matured flower rooted in the same spot where the Savior prayed. The flower of love...a rose...a single bloodred rose.

Twenty-six

Church

Bible Class

Jesus and George sit on the sofa, waiting on Martha. George looks at his watch. "Sweetheart, we don't want to be late."

"I'll be just another minute," she calls from the bedroom.

George looks to Jesus and shrugs his shoulders. "Women...! A good part of a husband's life is waiting."

Jesus shrugs his shoulders. "I wouldn't know," He says to George.

"That's right...oh, I'm sorry. I wasn't thinking. I didn't mean..."

"Don't sweat it, George. It's all right."

"I guess you were beyond all that," George remarks.

"No one is beyond love," Jesus says. "But it was for the sake of love I put such things aside."

Just then, Martha enters; the two men stand up.

"Well, I must say it was well worth the wait. You look very nice," Jesus tells her.

"Well, thank you."

"She is beautiful; isn't she?" George proclaims, smiling at her.

The three walk out the front door; George turns to lock up.

"You know, I must commend the two of you," Jesus says.

"How is that, Lord?" George asks.

"I'm just impressed both you and Martha have put the entire Bible to memory."

George slaps his own forehead as if struck with a revelation. "Our Bibles," George says. "We forgot our Bibles! I'll just pop inside and get them."

During the drive to church, George remains silent. He feels embarrassed. Not because he forgot their Bibles; but because in their laziness they no longer bothered to take their Bibles, there's a difference. He feels embarrassed because he tried to hide the fact. Worse, he tried hiding it from the one person you can't hide anything from. He knew Jesus knew. He knew Jesus knew that he knew that Jesus knew that...it is all so complicated. This is the uncomfortable part of having a close relationship with your Lord and Savior.

As they approach the church, Jesus breaks the silence. "Does your church have an adult Bible-study class?" He asks.

"Yes, we do," Martha replies. "George and I went to it once." The word "once" catches in her throat. It was a good class. Why did they not continue going? Now, it's her turn to feel embarrassed.

Looking at the clock on the dashboard, George says, "It starts in a few minutes. There are three services at our church. If you like, we can go to the class and then catch a later service?"

"Yes, I'd like that very much," says Jesus.

****

When they arrive, they hadn't started class, yet. There are just fewer than thirty people, mostly couples, standing about socializing.

"Donut…?" asks a stout little man, holding a donut in front of Jesus' face.

"Excuse me?" Jesus asks.

"Would you like a donut? There's plenty."

"Thank you; but no thank you."

"Jack Miller's the name, real estate's the game" the man says, shaking Jesus' hand. "I don't believe I caught your name."

"My name is Jesus."

"I don't remember ever seeing you here before?"

"I'm just here for the weekend, visiting friends."

"Well, if you ever think of settling here, I'm your man." Jack hands Jesus one of his business cards. "Great little community we've got here, low crime, good schools, great church…"

"Oh, so you like this church?"

"Sure do! It's a great place to network…if you know what I mean?" Jack shoves his elbow into Jesus' side, barely missing his wound. "It seems I make a new contact almost every week. Say, tell me, what line of work are you in?"

"I guess you could say I'm in salvage."

"Can't be much money in that; but I guess somebody has to do it!" Jack laughs, winks, poking his elbow again at Jesus. "Oh, look, class is starting; we better get a seat."

After everyone is seated, the leader stands at the front of the room, waiting for everyone to settle down. He opens class with a short prayer; and for the next hour, with Bible open, they delve into the scriptures. There are many questions, some answers, and even some debates. Jesus sits silently, smiling.

"I guess you can say I have a problem with all this Abraham and Isaac business," says a woman, holding her Bible and pointing to Genesis 22:2. "What I mean is…supposedly, our God is a loving God. He wants us to behave morally. Now, when you talk morals there are certain ones some people look at differently. Yet everyone has a conscience; there are certain things all of us can agree on – murder, for one. That's why, what I don't get is why God asks Abraham to kill his only, beloved son, as a sacrifice to Him?"

"However, God didn't let that happen. He stopped him at the last minute," says a man sitting behind her.

The woman turns in her seat to look behind her. "That's not the point!" demands the woman. "The point is what God is asking of Abraham to do doesn't sound so loving and unquestionably not moral. It seems illogical for God to test him this way…if you love me, you'll obey me, even if I tell you to do something that's wrong!"

A heavy silence hovers over the small group as each mind searches for the answer.

Jesus raises his hand; the group leader points to Him.

"I'm just a guest here, today. Nevertheless, if you'll allow me, I believe I can help." Jesus says.

"By all means, please," says the group leader.

Jesus stands and turns, facing the woman, speaking loud enough for all to hear. "You're correct in saying this was God's test for Abraham; only not for the reason you mentioned. The Father didn't need to test Abraham's love. No one loved the Father as much as Abraham; that's why the Father chose him above all others. It wasn't a test of obedience. When the Father said go to that foreign land, where you'll have no friends, no property, where you will be a nomad living in tents…Abraham went. Without a single question, without the batting of an eye, Abraham left behind his life and moved his family into Canaan.

"No, this was a test of faith. To believe everything the Father utters is true and good; and what He says will come to be…will be. This was where Abraham was weak…in his faith.

"The Lord promised Abraham a son. Except when more time than he was willing to wait passed, Abraham lost faith. He no longer believed in the Father's promise; so he decided to take matters into his own hands. Ishmael was conceived through Hagar, Sarah's maidservant. Years later when again he's promised a son and many descendants; his faith was weak. He and his wife laughed at the thought of it. But with the birth of his son, Isaac, he finally realized how feeble his faith was…how wrong he'd been.

"This was a test of faith! He knew the Lord promised many descendants through Isaac. He knew the Father would never let him kill his son. How could the bloodline continue as promised if his son were to die? He knew this was true; he just needed to prove he knew it was…to prove his faith…not to God, but to himself. He needed to get his priorities straight. Because, no matter what or whom you love in this world it should never be your first love. The Father must always come first!"

A deep reflective silence comes over the class. Finally, the silence is shattered.

"Wow, you almost make it sound like you were there!" someone hollers from the back of the room. The entire class bursts into laughter. Jesus smiles and sits down, again.

Twenty-seven

The Later Service

In church, George and Martha begin making their way to their usual seats in the back. Jesus takes another route and beelines to the front seats. George and Martha look at each other. They shrug their shoulders, smile, and follow.

The music minister steps up to the microphone, "Please stand and turn your Hymnals to page sixty-one...*It is well with my soul.*"

The congregation stands. Jesus turns slightly to see George and Martha staring at him.

"What...?" He asks; they remain silently staring. "What...?" He asks again; still mute and staring. "Do I have something in my teeth...what?"

"It's just that I've always wondered if Jesus Christ could sing; and if He could, what does his voice sound like?" George says.

"I'm used to singing in Hebrew, but it doesn't matter. As for my voice, I get by," Jesus answers. He takes a Hymnal, handing it to George, "Page sixty-one...It is well with my soul."

As the congregation sings, Jesus looks about the church. Everyone is dressed in their Sunday best. There are two things he notices that make him feel concerned. First, how few people are actually singing. Some are mouthing the words, not uttering a sound. Others are not even trying to fake it. They stand tightlipped. More women sing than men who stand at attention with their hands in their pockets. The other thing he notices is how few people are smiling. It almost seems to be an effort for them to be there. What should be a joyous sound comes across as a formality that one must trudge through.

After two more Hymns, everyone sits down, again. The organist makes her way to her seat, Pastor Jim steps to the pulpit. He places his Bible down, and he spreads a week's worth of notes out. He takes a moment to look out at the congregation. He looks left, then right, up and then down; his gaze stops on Jesus. His knees become weak, nearly giving out under him. He recognizes the man in the front row. He remains silent for what seems like an excessively long time. Whispers flood through the crowd; wondering what might be wrong. One of the elders stands, about to walk to him when the Pastor begins to speak – slowly at first.

"I worked all week preparing for today's sermon." Pastor Jim holds up a fistful of handwritten notes. "But I think it best we look at these another day. The Lord placed something on my heart just now; and I'm going to go with it." He raises his Bible. "If you could, please, open your Bibles to Matthew 28 verse 20."

The sound of pages turning fills the church.

"As always, we show our respect by standing for the reading of God's word."

They all rise; Pastor Jim waits for the rustle of the congregation to settle.

"Go to the last verse of this Gospel; and I want us all to read just the last line. In fact, we're not even going to read the last line to the end. Prepare to stop in an instant...this is going to be the shortest reading we've ever done...all together, now."

The entire church reads aloud as one voice, "And surely I am with you always..."

"Stop right there!" shouts Pastor Jim. "You may all sit down."

The congregation looks to one another, bewildered. This was not what they are use to or expect. Again, Pastor Jim waits for silence.

"And surely I am with you always," he repeats the phrase with deep emotion. "I want you to take your pens and underline the word *always*. Isn't that a wonderful word? Isn't it the best news you could hope for...always? The spirit of God isn't just with us sometimes; He's with us always! Not just when we pray or worship, but always. Even when He is the last person on our mind and the last person we expect." He stops for a moment to look at Jesus, and then he continues. "He never leaves us, even when we leave Him. He's always there...when we sleep...when we wake...when we're good...when we sin...always.

"Don't think just because he's not in the front of your mind you're not on His mind. He doesn't fly up to heaven whenever we stop thinking of Him and then come rushing back when we remember Him. He's there...always!"

Pastor Jim takes a hard, long look at his hands – examining his own flesh, his own humanness.

"We are such silly creatures. We only have five senses to make out the world. A common dog has more command over most of them than we do. Sometimes we forget there is something beyond our senses; that God is there with us...always.

"Here's a question. What if Jesus showed Himself to your five senses right now? I'm not talking about the *Second Coming*. I'm talking about Jesus showing up at your home or your office. He asks you what you've been up to; what would be your answer?"

By now, some of the congregation are nodding in understanding and smile, still, there are many who feel uneasy, squirming in their seats.

"If He were to ask you if your neighbors or co-workers were saved, could you tell Him? As for the ones not saved, could you tell Him what you've been doing about it?"

Some have stopped nodding and smiling.

If He wanted to look at your bankbook or checkbook, would you feel ashamed?"

Now there are far more people feeling uneasy than nodding and smiling. In fact, very few are smiling.

"Just because I'm your Pastor, doesn't let me off the hook. I'm no better or worse than the next person. If anything, I should know better, but I don't always act like I do. What if one Sunday I looked out and saw Jesus sitting in the front row? Would what I was saying please Him?"

Pastor Jim looks straight into the eyes of Jesus and smiles, "I hope He would be pleased." He places both hands on the pulpit. "So, what's my point? The point is this is not some make-believe fantasy story; it's as real as real can be. Forget what your five senses tell you: they're far too limited. The spirit of the Lord is always with us.

"Over the next week, why don't we…each of us…conduct an experiment? Take a small slip of paper and write the word *always* on it. Keep it in your pocket or purse; stick it on your refrigerator or your dashboard. Whenever you see it, may it remind you the Lord is with you. He's your partner in your life. And let's see how we act, and what decisions we make.

"If we stay mindful of Him, it can only change our lives for the better. So let the experiment begin; and I'm sure we'll have some fine testimonies next Sunday. Now, if you can all please stand and open your hymnals to number 192; let us join in singing that classic hymn *Always and Ever.*"

****

After service, Pastor Jim rushes head on into the thick of the crowd as they're leaving the church. He is just a few feet behind Jesus. He reaches out to touch Him when someone takes hold of his arm, placing their hand in his. It's dear Miss Mosley, an elderly woman, head of the church's senior club.

"Those were inspiring words you spoke today, Pastor," she shouts over the dim of the crowd.

"Thank you, Miss Mosley; I'm glad you liked it," he says not looking at her but keeping his eyes fixed on Jesus.

"Liked it…? It isn't a question of like; it was downright inspiring!"

"I'm glad you…" Pastor Jim's voice trails off as he watches the back of Jesus' head move farther and farther from him.

"Miss Mosley, please forgive me. I see someone I must speak with; it's especially important."

"A pastor's work is never done," she says, letting go of his hand.

"No, it isn't, thank you for being so understanding, Miss Mosley." He trudges on through the crowd. Again, he is a few feet behind Jesus when someone grabs him, stopping him.

"Great sermon, Jim; I don't know where you come up with this stuff." It's Carl Martin, one of the elders.

"Thanks, Carl. Say, listen Carl, I don't want to be rude, but I do have something important I need to look into."

The back of Jesus' head is drifting farther away as He approaches the church door. A few more steps, He will be gone.

"I understand," says Carl. "Just don't forget about that you-know-what."

Pastor Jim stops in his tracks.

"What are you talking about?"

"You know... the new heater for the church; we need to have a meeting."

"Yes, of course; I'll call you first thing in the morning," says Pastor Jim. He looks around; there is no sign of Jesus. He is too late.

Outside, Jesus and Martha wait at the steps of the church for George to bring the car around. Once inside the car, George asks, "So, what do you feel like?"

"I feel just fine, thank you," Jesus responds.

Martha clarifies the statement, "What do you feel like...it's just an expression. What George is asking is...What do you feel like eating? We usually like to go to a restaurant on Sundays after church, instead of going home to eat."

"You two know best; I leave it up to you," Jesus says.

"Well, if you're especially hungry," George says, "We can go to the 'Great Wall of China'; they've got a great buffet. Do you like Chinese food?"

"I don't know; I've never eaten any Chinese food."

"Why don't we just play it safe and go to *Clara's Country Kitchen*," Martha says.

"Good idea," George agrees, sounding a bit disappointed. There are images of egg rolls dancing in his head. Then he remembers the chicken-fried steak at Clara's Country Kitchen and all's right with the world once more.

"Which country are you talking about?" Jesus asks.

"It's not any particular country. It's a style of cooking. You know," Martha says. "Country, country, you know, down-home cooking."

"We're going to someone's home?" Jesus asks.

Martha feels like she's on a carousel. "You'll like it; trust me."

Twenty-eight

Sunday Afternoon

Tiffany

It's strange…you need a license to own a dog; but anyone can have a child, as many as you like, as often as you want. You must pass a test proving you can drive a vehicle safely on public roads, but you don't have to prove anything to anyone to have a child. You need a document from a reputable school to practice medicine or law. You need a license to fly a plane, own a gun, cut hair, give a massage, and hundreds of other pastimes and jobs. Nothing is needed to have a child other than the want. It is a basic human right.

Interesting, how many people feel the need to have a child, even if inwardly, if they were honest, don't want a child. Sad but true, not everyone should have a child. Dolly would be the first to admit raising children is not her strong point. She didn't have a green thumb in the garden. She was no cook; she burned everything in the kitchen. She never could hold a job for more than six months. She was still searching for her niche in life when she became pregnant.

"I guess you could say I had Tiffany just to rile my mother. I was always trying to please her or rile her. She was not a person you easily please. In fact, I don't think she was ever pleased with me. So, I decided to just rile her. It was easier," Dolly would laugh after her third beer. "Never married the father; he was a bum anyways…good riddance to bad news, I say."

Understandably, Tiffany's destiny was to be a Latchkey child. She seldom went to school, and when she did she felt alone and alienated. She never stepped inside a church. It wasn't until her teens someone explained what Christmas was about. It didn't make much sense to her, anyway. All she ever read were her mother's gossip magazines. She learned about love from the songs on the radio. She had few friends; and those she had were no better off than her, if not worse. She lived on peanut butter and jelly sandwiches. Now and then a half-full disregarded beer. Everything she learned or knew of the world was what she saw on the television. Her life was one of loneliness, without love, and eventually abuse. To her, the world was too terrible a place to bring a child into; at the early age of eleven, she swore never to marry or conceive.

Over the years, her mother hooked up with one man after another. Eventually, each in turn moved in. There was: Uncle Paul – Uncle Mike – Uncle Scooter – Uncle Jeff; not one staying longer than two years; that is until Uncle Geer. He moved in the year Tiffany turned fifteen. It was clear from the start Geer not only had eyes for Dolly but for Tiffany as well.

Some nights, Dolly and Geer drank themselves into unconsciousness on the couch. Some nights while Dolly slept it off, Geer snuck into Tiffany's room. The frightened girl couldn't do anything other than stare through tears at the ceiling.

She tried several times to tell her mother what was happening; Dolly refused to hear anything negative about "My Man" – as she liked to call him. "You're just making that stuff up because you're jealous. Because I've got somebody and you don't," Dolly scolded Tiffany, screaming, talking down to her like they were schoolmates and not mother and child.

Finally, just after her seventeenth birthday, one night when Dolly and Geer drank themselves into a deep stupor, Tiffany packed her bags. She took fifty dollars she saved from baby-sitting jobs, twenty-five dollars from the cookie jar, and three hundred dollars from Geer's wallet. She walked out, slamming the screened door, and never looked back.

She hoped to put all that behind her and start a new life. Once on her own, her life changed for the better. She could not and would not go back home. She braced herself, moving forward with her life as best she could. She believed life was just a series of bad events linked by short calm moments where you were allowed to catch your breath only to brace yourself to confront the next bad event.

Twenty-nine

The Restaurant

The waitress standing at the door smiles at Martha and George in recognition. They're regular customers.

"Three?" she asks in a perky tone.

"Yes, please."

She takes hold of three menus and guides them to a booth off in the corner, away from everyone else.

"Tiffany will be your waitress, today. She'll be right with you. Enjoy."

A young, dark-haired, teenage boy comes to them with a tray of three water glasses. He clumsily places the glasses on the table and rushes off.

They sit quietly reading their menus. George skims over the menu with little interest. He's already announced what he wanted, earlier.

"What's...Chicken-Fried Steak?" Jesus asks pointing to the menu. "Is it steak or is it chicken?"

Martha moves closer. "It's steak, but it's cooked as if it were chicken. It's very good."

"That's my favorite," George adds. "Smothered in country gravy, it's sheer heaven, although there's probably not a doctor in the country who'd recommend it as a healthy meal, starting with my doctor."

"What's your favorite?" Jesus asks Martha.

"Oh, I like the Chicken-Fried Chicken."

"And what's that?"

"It's chicken cooked as if it were a chicken-fried steak."

Jesus looks clearly confused. "But if it is chicken that's fried chicken-fried steak style, then it's not just like chicken fried steak with chicken, it is chicken fried chicken. Why don't they call it steak fried chicken?"

Somehow He makes sense, but it sends her head spinning. Martha feels safer in the kiddy pool, so she changes the subject. She reaches over, pointing to other items on Jesus' menu.

"Here's something I think you'll like."

"Catfish Platter..." Jesus reads. "That wouldn't be cat cooked as if it were a fish?"

"Oh, no..." Martha laughs. "That's just the name of the fish. There isn't an ounce of cat in it...I promise you."

A young woman, a teenager, approaches with her order pad. It's Tiffany; they know this by her nametag. "Good afternoon and welcome to Clara's. May I take your order?" She is small and slender. Her eyes are as dark as her short, black hair; but blackest of all is the cloud hanging over her. Her face is expressionless, unaffected by the trio of smiling faces. She takes their orders as if hearing them from a great distance.

Martha tries to help Jesus with his order. "Is that catfish breaded and fried or is it just plain and grilled?"

"You can order it either way, ma'am. It comes with Cole slaw and Hushpuppies."

Jesus laughs under his breath, "First cats, and now puppy dogs. I don't know about this."

"It's far better than it sounds. Trust me on this."

"Is it as good as the fish sticks?"

"It's far better than fish sticks!"

"Very well, I'll have the catfish and puppies."

The young woman writes down the order, and looks to George.

"I'll have the Captain's Plate with a glass of iced tea."

Martha looks at George in confusion. All that talk about chicken-fried steak, with a quick glance at the menu, he's changed his mind.

"I'll have the same. Make it iced tea for all of us," Martha adds.

"Fried or grilled?" asks the waitress.

"Fried," George announces without a second thought.

"Grilled, please," Martha says.

Clearly, the young woman's mind is far away; whatever sorrow she feels shows on her face. Holding the pad and pencil she walks off through swinging doors into the kitchen. She comes out carrying their drinks, placing them down, and then returning to the kitchen.

When the food arrives, George looks to Jesus, "Lord, this isn't our house; we'd feel blessed if you would say grace."

"If you wish," He says. They take one another's hands and bow their heads.

It's obvious a simple thing like saying grace causes a stir, heads turn, people whisper. Even some folks who normally say grace feel uncomfortable making such a fuss. Some people shake their heads in disagreement.

The young woman waiting on their table stands silent off to the side holding the straws Martha asked for. She waits for them to finish.

"Father, how great you are…how giving and loving. The earth is a bounty for all to share and it sings of your glory. We give thanks for every gift. We ask you bless this food, that it nourishes our bodies and minds to be instruments of Your Peace. Praise to you Father Almighty, Amen."

Jesus opens his eyes and sees the young waitress standing and watching. She's rolling her eyes, as many of the other costumers do. A look of uncomfortable embarrassment comes over her; she places the straws on the table near Martha, turns and rushes away.

****

"Would you like anything else?" asks the young woman, when it is clear they're finished. "Perhaps, some desert?"

"Oh, no; not me, I'm stuffed," George announces.

"No thank you, dear," Martha agrees.

She looks to Jesus for an answer. He smiles, reaches to Tiffany, taking her hand.

"What is your name, child?" He asks, despite her name tag.

She feels a strong impulse to pull away and run off; yet, she doesn't – she can't.

"Tiffany…" she answers. Again, she tries in her mind to run away; but she only stares into the eyes of Jesus. Never letting go of her hand, He speaks softly to her.

"His name was Thomas. As a baby the family called him 'Tom-Tom' until he turned eight when they called him 'Tommy'. When he became a man they called him 'Tom', and called him that till his dying day. Only his wife of forty-five years and his loving mother refused to call him anything but 'Thomas'.

"His mother, a single-parent, was too protective of him; something he later resented and rebelled against. Still, he remained a loving son till she died an old and gray-haired woman. After all, she was the one who God used most to save his soul. All her life she continued as an example to him…an example of goodness. From early prayers, to children's Bible stories read late at night. She read the Bible openly in her home. Through her, God directed efforts. By His Grace, Thomas was saved at the early age of ten.

'All his life he was a man others respected and loved. When he was well up in years, he became ill. As he died, surrounded by loved ones, his wife and grown children, he shed his skin with a smile and no fear."

The young woman is shaking; tears roll down her face, her hand tightens around his.

"Then you know him?" she asks.

Jesus reaches his free hand out to her, placing it on her belly.

"Yes, I know him…I have always known him and always will. I love him as the Father loves him and I will always love him. Even if all I told you does not come to pass, it will not affect the love I have for him…and for you.

"But I beg you, for his voice you cannot hear yet. Let these things come to pass. Let Thomas live!"

"I…I…" the young woman, unable to speak, unable to see through the tears, breaks free and runs into the kitchen, sobbing.

The entire room watches her flee in tears.

"The poor dear," one woman seated at another table says to her friend, "It's not easy being a waitress. I was one when I was just about her age." She looks across the room at Jesus. "Who knows what that guy said to her to make her cry like that!" She shakes her head. "Some people can be so cruel!"

Thirty

Mark

Mark was always full of good intentions; but he could never follow through with them. He never set out to do wrong or to do harm to anyone; though often that was the result. This was because of two main reasons. First, he never had good sense when it came to selecting his friends; he always chose from the bottom of the barrel rather than the top. Second, he was always easily swayed by those around him. This deadly combination was to be his downfall.

Even as a boy in school he surrounded himself with bullies, loudmouths, rebels, and braggarts. He would jump at any dare, regardless of the consequences.

After school, when he joined the Army, his parents hoped the military would straighten him out. Still, it was the same as it was back in school; he chose all the wrong friends. Despite getting into constant trouble, he barely made it through his stint and emerged with an Honorable Discharge.

Back home, Mark became a factory worker. He lived in a shabby, unkempt apartment. His appearance was scruffy. His debts mounted, bills went unpaid. Each paycheck went toward what Mark considered the Good Life. Again, this was all because of poor choices in friends and life-directions.

Thankfully, though none of us deserve it, there is such a thing as a second chance. That second chance Mark received in the form of a young, pretty, Godly woman named Kathy. Somehow, Kathy's eyes saw past the outer and fell in love with the inner Mark.

Mark's love for Kathy was so strong; he swore anything to have and keep her. Her goodness made him ashamed of what he was; he changed his ways. All those who cared for and loved Mark saw the change; and thanked God, hoping he finally became a responsible, grown man. As for his poor choices in friends, he didn't need to leave them, they left him. The change was so drastic that when he proposed to Kathy, she was glad to have him.

The first years of marriage couldn't have been happier for the both of them. Yet again, the call of the world became too strong for Mark. The voices of the wrong kind of friends and the call of wrong paths lead him astray. Within a year's time, the marriage looked hopelessly destine for divorce. It was time now, again, for another second chance. Mark had had his; this one was for Kathy. Her second chance came in the form of a baby...young Danny.

From the moment Mark held his son in his arms, with tears in his eyes, again, he swore to change. And he did, for a while; but Mark never possessed the strength to fight the pull of the world. No one does; a higher, stronger force is needed by all; but Mark knew nothing of such things.

Finally, after years of constant prayer, with her son's safety first in mind, Kathy asked Mark to leave, proceeding with divorce procedures. Mark was only too glad to leave to pursue the life he chose. Though inwardly he felt like a failure with a heavy aching in his heart, for he loved them both deeply. But pride leaves no room for much else.

On a Saturday night, sitting at the end of a bar at the local tavern, Mark kicked back a whiskey with a beer chaser. As his head tilted back, the room spun, everything went black; he fell off the stool and hit the floor with a thud. When he woke up he was in a bed at the VA hospital.

His prognosis was serious. In the weeks of being bedridden, the hospital Chaplin visited him daily. Again another chance was bestowed on Mark; this chance came in the form of his Savior – Jesus Christ.

Mark wrote letters to Kathy, telling her of his newfound life. All his letters returned unopened and unanswered.

It is never too late to receive the forgiveness of God. But people are not God. Understandably, Kathy had had enough.

Thirty-one

The Hitchhiker

"George, can you please head for the highway?" Jesus asks.

"But the highway doesn't take us home," George responds.

"I know; but there's something we need to do."

George knows better than to ask another question; he heads for the highway. They drive down Main Street till it ends at the on-ramp to the highway.

"There he is," Jesus says, pointing. "Do you see him? Slow down a bit."

At first, George and Martha have no idea what he's talking about till they see him. A young man sits on the curb of the on-ramp. As they slowly approach, he stands and sticks out his thumb. He's dressed in pajamas, a bathrobe, and slippers. George stops the car next to him and lowers the windows.

"Can we give you a ride?" George asks.

"Yeah, I'd appreciate it," says the young man, hopping into the backseat next to Jesus.

George looks in the rearview mirror at the young man. He's remarkably thin with dark circles under his eyes. His face needs a shave, his hair stands on edge, his skin is pale and pasty – the color of chalk.

"So, how far are you going?" George asks.

"I just need to get a couple of exits up…to Lancaster."

George catches the young man's eyes in the rearview mirror. "I don't mean to poke my nose into someone else's business, but I can't help noticing you're hitchhiking in your bedroom clothes."

A thousand lies run through Mark's mind. He is ready to say any one of them when he locks eyes with Jesus and finds he is unable to – he tells the truth – blunt and cold.

"I'm staying at the VA home off Main Street. I'm dying; I got some strange condition I still can't pronounce. It's weird dying of something you can't give a name to. I don't have long to live…weeks, days, hours…I don't know. My wife won't have anything to do with me. I don't blame her. I did her wrong so many times I can't count. I don't blame her at all. She won't talk to me and she won't let me talk with our son. I don't know what I'm doing out here. I guess, I just feel a need to say something to her and my boy before it's too late. Then I could die in peace. So I'm going home."

No one in the car feels a need to say another word. George takes the Lancaster exit.

"Now, which way…?" George asks.

The young man points, "Right over there; the first white house on your right."

George stops the car.

"I thank you folks for your kindness," says the young man; he hesitates. "Gee...now that I'm here, I don't know what I'm going to say to them."

Jesus places his hand on Mark's shoulder. "If you like, I could go in with you?"

Normally, Mark would decline such an offer. However, looking at the smile on Jesus' face, he cannot decline.

"Yes, thank you; that would be great."

Jesus and the young man exit the car and walk to the front door of the small white house. Mark looks inside through the screen door at the front of the house. He knocks; a minute passes, no one answers.

"Go ahead; go inside," Jesus says.

Mark opens the door; they enter. Looking around, the small home is neat and calm. They follow sounds coming from the kitchen. A young woman is there, preparing dinner; off in the corner, playing on the floor with a handful of green plastic toy soldiers is a small boy.

"Kathy! Don't' be mad at me...I've come home. Danny...it's me...Daddy!" says Mark. The young woman continues her cooking; the boy continues playing. He turns to Jesus, "They can't see or hear me. Am I already dead?"

"Not yet," Jesus whispers. "Their hearts can hear you; speak to their hearts."

Mark walks over and stands next to his wife. Like an unseen ghost, he gently speaks to her.

"Kathy...I know you're mad at me; and I don't blame you. I've been such a fool. I know I've hurt you. I hope someday you'll find it in your heart to forgive me. I hope someday you find a good man to marry; someone who deserves a fine woman like you. I hope someday you see past all my foolishness and know I loved you."

The woman stops what she's doing and stares off as if hearing a voice from afar off shore.

He turns and moves over to the small boy.

"Danny...son...there's so much I want to say to you; there's so much I want to share, but there isn't any time. So, I'll make it brief and say just what's most important. "I love you more than life itself. No matter what they may say about your old man, know I loved you. Listen to your mother. Grow strong, be your own man. Follow what's right even when others around you call you a fool. Treat your mother and all women with respect. Keep from bad company. Hold your body and loved ones in high esteem and never mistreat either one.

"If I'm ever to be anything to you, let me be a shining example of what a man must not become. Be happy. I hope someday you can look past my faults and know I love you. I love you."

The small boy stops, places his toys down and looks towards his father. He sees nothing, yet feels the presence of something unseen.

"Mom, did you hear something?"

"It's okay, baby...it's okay."

Mark walks to the door of the kitchen and stands next to Jesus; he addresses his family one last time. They remain motionless, listening to words their ears cannot hear.

"The next time you hear of me, I guess it will be I've passed on. I guess that's probably best for all of us. Outside the loss of you two, it doesn't bother me. Somehow, amid my foolishness and sinfulness, I found Jesus Christ; and though I know I could never deserve it, I'm bound for heaven.

"I guess that's the last and most important thing I could say to you both. There is one-way, and that way is Jesus. If you don't know that, I pray someday you do."

With that, the young man turns to Jesus. "I'd like to leave now," he says softly.

The drive back up the highway is a solemn journey; no one speaks a word. When they approach the on-ramp where they found him, Mark places his hand on George's shoulder.

"You can leave me where you found me."

"No, that's all right," George says. "We can take you to the VA home."

"No, this is fine. It isn't far, and I'd enjoy the walk. Thank you, again. You don't know what this means to me. Thank you."

The car stops; Mark gets out and looks at Jesus sitting in the backseat.

"I'll be seeing you?" The young man's statement sounds more like a question.

Jesus smiles ever so slightly. "Yes, I'll be seeing you."

"Soon...?"

Jesus reaches out the window, placing his hand on Mark's. "No man knows the hour; but I promise we will be together again in paradise."

The young man breaks into a weak but obvious smile. He slowly pulls away from Jesus' grip, turns and walks off.

Thirty-two

Sunday Evening

Jesus sits on the living room sofa reading the Bible. George sits across from him in a large arm chair reading his Bible.

"George, what are you doing?" Jesus asks without looking up.

"Why…I'm reading the Bible, Lord."

"I know that, George. Only *why* are you reading it?"

The question takes George aback; there's a moment of silence as he regroups his thoughts before he answers. He thinks of all the reasons he's been told reading the Bible is a good thing. He has to pick one.

"I read it to learn more and grow in God's word." An excellent answer as far as George can tell.

Jesus closes his Bible and smiles at George. "Even though you can't keep your mind off the big game playing on the television, yet, you still want to read your Bible? Even knowing the game has only fifteen more minutes to go; and you're itching to run to the set and see who is going to win, you still want to read your Bible?" Jesus holds up his Bible, looks at George, and smiles. "You know, George. Just because I'm sitting here reading the Bible does not mean you have to. There's no need to try to impress me. I know you're serious about your Bible reading."

"I wasn't trying to impress you." Instantly, George catches what he said and back steps. "Well, guess I was…just a little," he says shyly.

Jesus opens His Bible, holding it up to George. "Does this book scare you? It shouldn't. The Father wrote it to be People-Friendly, or should I say…Child-Friendly. The main objective isn't to fill your head; it's to fill your heart. Be religiously unreligious. What's most important is the connection between the two of us. Right now, our connection is strong enough to withstand you taking the next fifteen minutes to see who wins the big game." Jesus bobs his head, pointing his chin toward the next room. "Now, go ahead; enjoy the game."

George closes his Bible and runs away, smiling like a young boy who received permission to go outside and play. Suddenly, he stops at the door and looks back at Jesus

"Lord?"

"Yes, George."

"Do you know who's going to win the big game?"

"You're going to miss it, George."

George leaves the room, smiling, Jesus smiles, returning to his Bible.

****

"Is anyone hungry, yet?" Martha asks, poking her head into the living room. She finds Jesus alone. "Where's George?"

"He's watching the big game."

Just then George enters, dragging his feet, his shoulders slumped, his head down. "They lost," he moans.

"Oh, George, sweetheart, I'm sorry to hear that," Martha says, clearly out of sympathy – she never cared for sports nor was she able to tell one team from another.

The door bell rings.

"Now, I wonder who that could be, at this hour?" asks George, wearing a questioning look as he walks to the front door. He looks out the window. "It's Pastor Jim!" he exclaims. George looks to Jesus for guidance.

"That's fine, George," Jesus says. "Let him in."

George opens the front door only slightly; just enough to show his smiling face.

"Pastor Jim, what a pleasant surprise."

The pastor presses the flat of his right hand against the door. "George...is He here?"

"Is who here?"

"George...please...I need to speak with Him!"

"But...but..." George stumbles over his tongue.

"It's fine, George." Jesus is standing behind George. He gently places his hand on George's shoulder, guiding him away; with his other hand He opens the door.

Pastor Jim rushes into the room, falling to the floor at Jesus' feet – trembling, unable to speak. Jesus falls to his knees next to him, taking him in his arms. Pastor Jim begins sobbing.

"It's all right, Jim," Jesus whispers, "I know why you're here."

Pastor Jim takes a minute to control his emotions. He backs slightly away from Jesus, enough to look into his face. "You...do...?"he asks

"Of course, I do," Jesus says, helping him to his feet. Jesus continues to hold Jim by his arms, looking straight into his face with deep concern.

"She's so sick. She's been sick for so long. It just seems to be getting worse. I don't know what to do. I can't stop thinking about her," Pastor Jim weeps uncontrollably. "I try to do my job, I write the sermons, but it's all mechanical. I preach the Gospel, but it's just empty words. I listen to the troubles of others...people who need my guidance...and all I can give them is textbook answers. All I can think about is my wife, Darcy, and how ill she is and how terrible she must feel." He stops for a moment and takes a deep swallow. "I realize she's dying. She knows it, too. She's so brave. You wouldn't know it to speak with her. She never complains.

"Part of me wants her to die...and soon...so she'll no longer suffer. Another part of me wants her to live so I can have her with me just a little longer. Either way, I can't believe how selfish I am."

Jesus pulls him in close, tightens his arms around him and whispers in his ear, "You're doing just fine, James, just fine."

Pastor Jim takes a full breath, trying his best to remain calm. "Matthew 9:20 tells us of a woman ill for years who knew just the touch of the hem of your garment would heal her."

Jesus backs away slightly, looking into James' eyes. Knowing the question, He still waits for the asking, before He answers.

"Lord, God Almighty, have mercy. Come with me to the hospital. Let Darcy touch the hem of your garment, let her too receive healing!"

Jesus nods and smiles.

"Do you want us to come, too?" George asks.

"Yes, I think you both can help," Jesus says.

George and Martha wonder what He could mean. How could they ever be of any help?

They lock the house and rush to the cars, George and Martha in one car, Jesus rides with Pastor Jim. They speed off into the night to the hospital.

Thirty-three

Leo and Cameron

"Yes…all right, I'm coming," Leo scolds the front door buzzer as he turns the knob, opening the door.

It's Cameron. He comes bursting in uninvited, waving a sheet of paper in the air. "Sorry to bother you like this, Leo; we've just got to talk. This thing is driving me crazy."

"No bother, I know all about *crazy*," says Leo lackadaisically. "So, what's driving *you* crazy?"

"This!" He shoves the list of religions everyone put together at the picnic.

"Oh, that," says Leo with a sly grin. "What about it?"

"Well," says Cameron, "it has allowed me to understand the uniqueness of Christianity and why a Christian believes Christ is the only way; but it doesn't disprove the other belief systems. How can you say one is right and all the others are wrong?" He points to the long list of religions on the one side of the paper, opposite Christianity.

The grin leaves Leo's face. "Do you like beer, ginger ale, or cola?" he asks.

Cameron looks at him in a moment of silent astonishment, before he speaks. "I may have just asked you the most important question of my life, and you want to know what I want to drink!"

Leo's expression doesn't change. "So what is it…beer…ginger ale…or cola?"

Cameron gives into his whim. "Neither…bottled water's all I drink."

"That figures," says Leo. He walks passed Cameron, making his way to a door under the stairs leading to the basement. Leo hollers toward the kitchen, "Honey, our neighbor Cameron is here. We're going to go downstairs and play some pool."

"That's nice, dear," Dianne's response is polite, calm and classical. If he said Genghis Khan just arrived with a heard of elephants and wanted to set up camp in the backyard, her reply would have been the same.

As Leo takes hold of the doorknob leading to the basement, Cameron seizes Leo's arm. "My soul is on fire and you want to play pool?"

Leo looks deep into Cameron's eyes before speaking. "Believe me, if you want to learn anything, you and I need to play a game of pool."

Making no sense to Cameron at the time, he follows orders; the two make their way down to the basement playroom. At the bottom of the stairs, Leo flicks a wall switch; the florescent lights dangling above the pool table hum and flicker until fully lit. Leo opens an old fridge leaning against the wall; bottles clank as he rummages about.

"Sorry…no bottled water; you sure I can't talk you into at least a ginger ale?"

"No, I'm not thirsty, thank you," Cameron says sounding slightly belligerent.

"You don't mind if I have one?"

"No, of course I don't; I'm just not thirsty."

"But you do get thirsty?" asks Leo as he twists the cap off a cola.

"What a strange question. Of course, I get thirsty!"

Leo takes a gulp and smiles, "What if I told you about a well that once you taste its water you'll never be thirsty again."

Cameron looks at him sideways, through squinted eyes and with tight pressed lips, as if to say the question didn't deserve an answer.

"I don't blame you," says Leo, "I didn't believe it when I first heard it. I guess you can say it's an inside joke…a joke I'm praying you someday get." Leo places his soda down and starts racking the pool balls. "You any good at playing pool?"

Cameron shakes his head, "I don't think I've played more than two games my whole life."

"Good," Leo smiles, "cause I stink at it. I only play it because it relaxes me. Why don't we start off with a few games of straight pool…nothing fancy. Mind if I break?"

"Leo…I don't even know what that means!" Cameron tosses the page onto the green felt. He points to the long list of religions.

Leo picks up the list, examining it once more. "Before we start, I've got one important question."

Cameron waits for the other shoe to drop, but it doesn't. "Okay, you have a question, what is it?"

"Before we start, I want to know how serious you are. Are you just looking for me to confirm what you already believe, or do you have an open mind. Most people are blinded by what they expect to see. What I mean to say is, if I give you cold hard facts you can't dispute, will you accept them?"

"Of course, I will."

"Good, cause I don't want to waste my time and yours."

Cameron tries to remain calm. "Leo…please, explain to me what's wrong with all these other religious systems."

Leo takes a long draw from his soda bottle. "I was just coming to that; only first I need to ask you perhaps the strangest question anyone ever asked you."

Another question! Cameron thinks. He straightens his stance, preparing for the worst. "Go ahead, ask away."

Leo places down his soda and shifts his weight to one side, leaning on his cue stick. His smile grows wide, almost ear to ear. "Can you tell me what *Thought* is?"

The question takes Cameron aback. "Why, that's easy. Everyone knows *Thought* is…well it's like…I mean when you're thinking…and you have thoughts…and…" Cameron stops and smiles at Leo. "You know, to be honest, I don't know. I do it ever waking minute of the day, thinking, that is. I'm doing it right this moment, but I can't express what it is."

Leo's smile leaves his face. He doesn't want Cameron to feel belittled by his answer.

"Thought is our mind's reaction to all stimuli in our world." He waves his hands over the racked colored balls. "Think of these balls as your world." He points to each ball individually. "This is your wife, these are your kids, and this is your job, politics, friends, family, and all other such nonsense we must contend with. Now, tell me how do you contend with this world? What instrument do you use?"

Cameron catches on immediately and smiles, "Why…with my mind…like you said."

"Good," says Leo, "Now, tell me where the mind gets its reactions from?"

The smile leaves Cameron's face. He feels stuck, again.

Leo holds up the single white cue ball. "Why…from your memory."

"Yes, of course," the smile returns to Cameron.

"Now here's the next big question," Leo asks with excitement in his voice, "What is memory?"

Cameron looks off for a longtime, thinking of an answer. It takes him a moment; again his smile returns to him. "I've got it!" he shouts. "Memory is a collection of experiences stored in the person's mind!"

"Excellent!" says Leo. He places the white cue ball down on the table. "We interact with our world by using our mind, which is a storeroom of memories." Suddenly, he picks up the white cue ball, again. "If memory is the content of the mind…If you have no memory you have no thought, correct?"

"Correct," responds Cameron.

Leo places the cue ball down once more. "With our experienced filled minds we have an instrument to react to our world." Leo pulls back on his cue stick and with one swoop hits the cue ball that slams into the cluster of racked balls. The balls scatter to every end of the table; two of them even find their way into a pocket.

"Great shot," says Cameron, not knowing if it in fact was; just feeling it's the thing to say.

"Not bad," replies Leo, "but not a great shot. The object of the game is to hit the cue ball into the colored balls, causing them to fall into the pockets. If it were truly a *Perfect Shot* all the colored balls would be in one of the pockets."

"But that's impossible," Cameron tries to point out.

"Why's it impossible?" snaps Leo. "I used the correct system. I hit the cue ball into the racked balls. I was successful to a point. But for all purposes, I failed; and I'll explain why." He picks up the white cue ball and holds it out to Cameron who takes it. "Thought is a reaction to our world, by our minds through our memories, which is a collection of our lifetime experiences. Those experiences are always limited…they must be. No matter if you live twenty minutes or live to be one hundred and twenty, your life experiences are limited.

"Even if you believe in reincarnation, which I don't; it still doesn't add up. If you live a hundred lives…a thousand lives…a million lives…you still only have limited experience. You cannot be, and never will be, all knowing."

"Let me see if I get this straight," says Cameron. "Thought is the mind's reaction from memory, which is a collection of experiences that are always limited no matter how noble they may seem or how many there are. So, that means all the thoughts of everyone are limited." He runs his hand down the list of religions once more. "That means whatever system a man may come up with for salvation, no matter how righteous or holy it might seem it must always be limited and incomplete – falling short."

"That's it in a nutshell," smiles Leo.

"But then what's the difference with Christianity?"

Leo points to the list of religions, "All these religions…these systems…were formed by good and well-meaning men…but men nonetheless, just like you and me…limited." Then he points to the lone word *Christianity* written on the other side of the paper. "Christianity isn't even a system, as we established before; it's a relationship with the all-knowing, unlimited, perfect, loving God."

Cameron looks lost in thought. "Say, Leo, does that Ginger Ale offer still stand?"

"Of course it does, buddy."

Leo takes out two more soda bottles, handing one to Cameron. "You still feel like playing pool?"

Cameron takes a long swallow of Ginger Ale. "No, but if you don't mind, I'd like to hear the story about that *well* you spoke about."

Thirty-four

The Hospital

Coming out of the elevator, the small group walks to the information counter, except for Pastor Jim, at the head of them; he rushes. There are two nurses on duty. The older, senior nurse steps forward. The others arrive in time to hear her speak to Pastor Jim.

"I'm sorry, but it's far too late, past visiting hours, for me to allow you to enter her room," says the nurse looking sympathetic. "Besides, she's sleeping; we've finally got her to sleep."

"I am her husband," says Pastor Jim. "It'll only be for a minute."

"I'm sorry; sir, but these are the hospital rules."

"We only want to look in on her for a minute." There is such desperation in Pater Jim's voice.

The nurse hesitates. "Well…just for a minute…if you promise not to wake her."

"I promise."

They back away from the front desk; the nurse stops them. "I'm afraid I can't allow all four of you at the same time."

George places his hand on Martha's shoulder. "That's fine. Martha and I can wait out here; you two go ahead."

Martha smiles at Pastor Jim. "Don't worry; we'll be praying."

"Can we two see her?" Pastor Jim asks pointing to himself and then Jesus standing at his side.

Again, the nurse hesitates. She looks to the other nurse; she's busy at her computer. "I suppose it will be all right," she finally decides.

George and Martha go to a waiting area and sit down. Jesus and Pastor Jim turn and start down the hall.

Pastor Jim stands bedside looking at his sleeping wife. Darcy's breathing is shallow and irregular. Her head has wires attached on all sides; tubes of clear liquid run from plastic bags into her arms, another tube runs down into one nostril. An electronic beep ticks off her heartbeat. He holds out his arms, desperately wanting to fall on her and take her in his arms; but afraid to wake her. His arms slowly return to his sides; with tears in his eyes he turns, looking hopefully toward Jesus.

"Tell me, James," Jesus asks, "what have you done for her?"

A confused look sweeps over Jim's face. "Lord, you know the hours I've spent on my knees praying."

"What did you pray for?"

"I prayed…for a miracle…for my wife to be spared!"

"Praying for the benefit of others is praiseworthy. I ask you, James, what have you done for her?"

Jim's hands reach out to Jesus. "Lord, I don't understand!"

Jesus closes his eyes as he speaks. "James…James…where is your faith?" He opens his eyes, again. "With faith anything is possible if asked in My Name. Have you commanded Satan to release his hold on your wife…in My Name? Have you rebuked the disease in her body…in My Name? What demands have you made…in My Name?

"Prayer is blessed communion…obedience gives strength…but faith is power! James…James…where is your faith?"

In silence, Jesus turns and leaves the room. Jim falls to his knees and begins crying tears of joy. The worry and despair held in his heart for such a long time vanishes. He stands and gently places his hands on his beloved wife.

"In the Name of our Lord and Savior, Jesus Christ…I…"

Thirty-five

Sunday Night

Jesus sits alone on the couch; George is in the armchair across from him.

"Does anyone want some ice-cream?" Martha calls from the kitchen.

"None for me, honey," George replies over his shoulder.

"No thank you, Martha," Jesus says. He looks George squarely in the eye. "George, the weekend is over; I need to leave."

George stares blankly.

"I want you to call the City Cab Company and order a cab to take me to the airport."

George nods, rises from his chair, and enters the kitchen. He finds Martha leaning against the sink, savoring a bowl of ice-cream.

"He's leaving," George says softly. Martha places her unfinished bowl of ice-cream in the sink. "He says the weekend is over, and He needs to leave."

George walks to the wall phone and removes the receiver.

"What are you doing?" Martha asks.

"He wants me to call for a cab to take Him to the airport."

"That doesn't make any sense," Martha shrieks. "Why would the Lord need a cab to take Him to the airport? For that matter, what would the Lord need with an airport?" Martha flies out of the kitchen.

She stands before Jesus, "Lord, George tells me you're leaving."

George enters the room, "City cab says they have a cab in the area; he'll be here in a minute."

"Lord...?" Martha persists.

"That's right, Martha, I'll be leaving." He exits to his room for a moment, returning holding the Bible Martha gave him in hand.

"Is it something we said...something we did?" Martha pleads.

"No, it's just the end of the weekend. You and George have been gracious hosts."

"If you want, we could drive you to the airport?" George asks.

Jesus smiles and laughs slightly. "George...Martha...by now you know I have no need for a cab or an airport. But, I do want to talk with Clifford...that's the cabdriver. The airport is just the distance I need to speak with him."

Just then, the doorbell rings. George opens the door and sticks his head out, "It'll be just another minute, Clifford."

"Hey...?" says Clifford in confusion to a now-closed door.

"Isn't there anything we can say or do to make you stay?" Martha begs.

Jesus takes her hand; George stands behind Martha, his hand on her shoulder.

"George…Martha….haven't you two learned anything? Do you think I arrived here at your door three days ago and now I'm going to leave in a taxi? I was here before and I remain after. As Pastor Jim said, 'I am with you always.'"

"May I give you a hug good-bye?" Martha asks shyly.

"Well…only if it comes with a kiss."

She hugs him, gently kissing his cheek; tears roll down her face.

George extends his hand, but he's pulled into a hug by Jesus. "Love one another as I have loved you," He whispers.

George opens the door. Clifford is still standing there. "Say, how did you know my name was Clifford?"

Jesus steps forward. "Why, Clifford, don't you remember me?"

The cabbie looks Him up and down, "I don't think so."

"You will," Jesus says. "We'll talk about it on the way to the airport."

"So, where's your luggage?" Clifford asks.

"Just this," Jesus says, holding up his Bible.

Clifford rolls his eyes, "Great…that's all I need!"

Martha and George stand at the doorway watching them walk to the cab.

"Mind if I sit up in the front with you?" Jesus asks.

"As long as you pay your fare, I don't care if you sit on the hood."

George and Martha bend low to get one last look at Jesus. He waves to them. When the cab disappears into the distance, they enter, George closes the door. Silently, Martha goes to the kitchen, opens a drawer, takes out a pen and paper. When she's done writing, she tapes the page to the front of the refrigerator. George walks over to see what she wrote. It's only one word…*ALWAYS.*

Thirty-six

Saturday Morning

Two Weeks Later

"Bills...bills...and more bills; nothing ever changes," George insists as he eyes the morning mail, seated at the kitchen table in front of his morning coffee. He catches the aroma of something unexpected; he turns to Martha. "Is that meat loaf I smell? Are we having meat loaf for breakfast?"

"No, silly," Martha laughs. "This is something I'm cooking for the Pastor and his wife. Darcy's finally home; but she's still bedridden. Some of the women at the church decided to bring meals. Today's my turn; I'm making meat loaf."

"Hmmm...smells good. How about you give them the rest of last night's tuna noodle casserole and we keep the meat loaf?" George laughs.

Martha shoots him a look.

"Okay...okay...I'm just kidding," George confesses. Martha is still looking sharply at him. "No...really...honestly...I was just kidding!" he says, his hands raised high. Martha returns to her cooking, George to opening the mail. He places one of the envelopes down on the table. "Say, what do we have here?"

Martha stops what she's doing, stepping to the table, looking at the envelope. "It's addressed to us; the lettering is in gold. You don't think...?"

"I don't know what to think," George says, "Why don't you open it and see?"

"No...my hands are too wet."

"Then dry them off."

She takes a towel and dries her hands, shaking her head, "No, I can't; you open it, George."

"For Pete's sake," he grumbles as he takes the letter. He opens it and begins reading a card. "What's it say, George?"

He begins to smile; slowly the smile turns to laughter. "It's an invitation to a wedding...from Tommy and Trish...you know, those two kids from down the block."

"How sweet of them to remember us," Martha coos.

"How could they not; they became engaged in our backyard."

"That is true," she laughs. "You know, when I first saw the gold lettering, I though it was from you-know-who."

"I know you did...because I thought the same."

"Aren't we silly," Martha giggles, pointing to the one word note on the refrigerator.

"Silly, indeed," George laughs. "Always…He's with us always." He jumps from his chair, taking her in his arms. "Always…just like you and me, my love…always!" He's just about to kiss her when the air becomes serrated by the blast from a lawn mower.

"That man…every Saturday morning like clockwork." Martha says.

George nuzzles his wife's neck till she screams with laughter.

"You mean the little man from across the street… that guy across the street in the Bermuda shorts and the silly black socks, him with his ridiculously loud lawn mower?"

"Yes!" she squeals in laughter as he snuggles harder.

"You mean the guy with the saggy, knobby knees, who wakes the entire neighborhood every Saturday morning?"

"Yes…stop, let me catch my breath," she shouts; tears of laughter run down her cheeks.

He lets go of her, opens the refrigerator, taking out two cans of cold soda pop.

"Mowing a lawn can be thirsty business. Let me just ask our neighbor what his name is and if he'd like to know our names. And if he has a name, and he wants to know who we are, I'm going to ask him if he knows Jesus Christ."

Martha wipes her eyes with her apron. George turns. "George…?" she calls him back. "I love you."

With a soda can in each hand, he motions to the *Always* note on the refrigerator, winking at her. "It's you and me, babe."

She watches from the window; she sees George approach the little man. He turns off his mower; the two men speak for a moment and then shake hands. George hands one of the cans to the little man. They pop open the cans, take a few sips, and then continue to talking. She can't hear what they're saying, she can only imagine. She feels tears once again welling up in her eyes. "That's my boy."

Martha sits down to finish her coffee. She looks at the next unopened letter on the top of the pile of mail. She reads the return address – *Christ the King Adoption Agency*. Her hands shake with anticipation as she opens the letter.

THE END

Michael Edwin Q. is available for book interviews and personal appearances. For more information contact:

Michael Edwin Q.
C/O Advantage Books
P.O. Box 160847
Altamonte Springs, FL 32716
michaeledwinq.com

Other Titles by Michael Edwin Q:

But Have Not Love: 978-1-59755-494-7
Pappy Moses' Peanut Plantation: 978-1-59755-482-8
Born A Colored Girl: 978-1-59755-478-4
Twilight Zone for Christians: 978-1-59755-463-3

To purchase additional copies of these book visit our bookstore website at:
www.advbookstore.com

Longwood, Florida, USA
"we bring dreams to life"™
www.advbookstore.com

CPSIA information can be obtained
at www.ICGtesting.com
Printed in the USA
FFHW010151040319
50802303-56216FF